AMERICAN UNIONS

Structure, Government,
and Politics

STUDIES

IN LABOR

Consulting Editor,

HENRY DAVID
NATIONAL ACADEMY OF
SCIENCES

AMERICAN UNIONS

Structure, Government and Politics

BY

JACK BARBASH

University of Wisconsin

RANDOM HOUSE · NEW YORK

PREFACE

In this book I have sought to study unions as a governmental system. I have, consequently, (1) outlined the formal features of the several levels of union government; (2) sketched the evolution of government at each of these levels to its present state; (3) assessed the forces at work in the evolution of government; (4) located the forms and functions of government in the context of the union as a whole; (5) shown how people and politics affect government in action; (6) indicated the interrelationship between public and union law; and (7) considered union government in terms of such analytic concepts as constitutional government, sovereignty, separation of powers, due process, and bureaucracy.

Above all I have tried, on the one hand, to show the relevance of union government to the larger forces at work in the economy and to the values and processes of a democratic society and, on the other, to communicate the significance of Walter Lippmann's observation, made more than fifty years ago, that "the effort to build up unions is as much the work of pioneers as the extension of civilization in the wilderness."

The Graduate School Research Committee of the University of Wisconsin has made possible financial support and research time at various stages in the preparation of this book.

The debt to my wife, Kate Barbash, for her work on this book continues to mount with no prospect in sight for repayment or amortization.

JACK BARBASH
University of Wisconsin

Madison, September, 1965

CONTENTS

AMERICAN UNIONS
*Structure, Government,
and Politics*

CHAPTER I

Introduction

The way unions are governed takes on fuller meaning if their general function in the industrial environment is understood, for the contemporary union may be viewed primarily as a response to modern industrialism. This term signifies the technological and managerial disciplines associated with the rational organization of work for the mass production of goods and services. Central to modern industrialism is the principle of rationality in the planning of enterprise decisions according to some cost-output standard. The application of this principle introduces tensions and strains in the management-worker relationship whenever it leads to decisions which in the eyes of workers conflict with their interest in job security, work satisfaction, and sense of equity. In an industrial economy, worker protest of some organized sort is unavoidable, and the union is a special and perhaps the most advanced form of worker protest. There is, in fact, a symbiotic relationship between the highly developed forms of industrial capitalism and the highly sophisticated forms of unionism. Developing industrialism in avowedly socialist economies has not yet generated the form of autonomous unionism found in Western capitalist economies.

Even in advanced industrial societies organized worker protest need not take the form of unionism.[1] In the United States, for example, less than one-fourth of the labor force is unionized and probably less than half of the actual potential for unionization has been realized.

When worker protest assumes the form of a union, its paramount objective is to conclude a formal bargain with management over the terms of employment. The incentive for management to conclude such a bargain lies in the fact that the workers will collectively withhold their labor until an agreement is reached. The workers' incentive lies in their immediate need for the income which the jobs provide. The power and the right of each party to withhold what the other side needs are basic to collective bargaining. When agreement is reached, a written contract establishes the terms of employment as enforceable rights, and creates a joint union-management system for interpreting the meaning of these rights in the day-to-day job problems. More often than not, this joint system—commonly spoken of as a grievance procedure—embraces a mechanism for impartial arbitration, with the decisions being binding upon the union and management.

Both functionally and historically, union organization is based upon the local union. This is the organization which brings together workers in a common trade or industry within a fairly compact or coherent geographic area. Thus, the local union may contain workers at one worksite or at several, employed by one or more employers. In the evolution of union forms the "trades union"—later known as the central labor body—developed after the appearance of local unions. In the United States, the contemporary central labor body in a city brings together diverse locals belonging to national unions, affiliated with the AFL-CIO, for common legislative and political interests. Such interests provide the basis for state-wide federations of labor unions.

With the emergence of the national union—or the international union, in recognition of affiliated local bodies in Canada*—the workers' potential organizational power

* Hereafter the term "national" union will designate both national and so-called international unions.

was extended enormously. Moreover, national federations of labor of an enduring character were formed. The federation as a national association of unions for legislative and political objectives had its origins in the early decades of the nineteenth century. However, it did not achieve its present form until the founding of the American Federation of Labor in 1886. Today, the AFL-CIO, a merger of the AFL and the rival Congress of Industrial Organizations founded in 1935, is the dominant national federation.

Collective bargaining is the core function of American unions. Auxiliary, supporting, and derivative functions include the organizing of new unions, the governing and administration of the union, the handling of strikes, and such external functions as participation in political activities and representation in governmental bodies.

The starting point for understanding the union as government is the operational fact that every union has a work territory covering a specified geographic area or, more commonly, a "jurisdiction" over which it asserts a special interest. A pioneering scholar wrote more than a half-century ago, "Just as one cannot imagine the existence of a government without an area over which it exercises control, so one cannot think of a trade union without assuming at the same time that there is a territory over which it claims jurisdiction." [2]

Union structure in a restricted sense refers to the type of jurisdiction. If the jurisdiction is narrowly defined in terms of a skill, craft, or occupation, its structure is classified as "craft." If the jurisdiction is broadly defined in terms of an industry or group of industries, its structure is classified as "industrial." The classic craft unions are found, for example, in building trades, railroads, and printing trades. The classic industrial unions are the mass production unions in coal, steel, automobiles, rubber, and the like. In reality, however, there are few or no "pure" structural types. It is difficult, if not impossible, to find a pure craft union or a pure industrial union. Moreover, union structure may also be classified according to the scope of the employer unit with which the union bargains, in which case the basic types are single-employer or multi-employer.

Another key reference point for delineating the union as government is the fact that workers have almost as many differences with each other as they have with their employers. The differences among the former stem mostly, but not exclusively, from disagreement over their job interests. Jurisdiction, therefore, provides an orderly basis for deciding which union's job interests shall prevail in the event of a contest between unions. Differences in interest among workers, consequently, are the basis for a continuously functioning political process within the union. Thus, much of the time of union leaders is taken with asserting or conciliating interests among groups of workers or, to put it another way, in participating in the political process.

The third key reference point is recognition of the existence of a dual system of union government. One is based in the shop and centers on collective bargaining with the employer. The other is based in the union hall and centers on the internal management of the union as an institution. However, because so much of the union's function and activity revolve around collective bargaining, the two systems of government are in constant and close interaction.

CHAPTER II

Jurisdiction and Structure
of American Unions

The operating import of jurisdiction is that it marks off the work claim of one union as against the claim of other unions.[1] In this sense jurisdiction is a product of the "scarcity consciousness" of the worker[2] and represents a protective device which groups of workers (whether in unions or not) have long used to establish their exclusive quasi-property right in custom and law to practice a particular craft:[3]

> To the member of a Craft Guild or Incorporated Company it seemed as outrageous, and as contrary to natural justice, for an unlicensed interloper to take his trade as for a thief to steal his wares. [According to the Emperor Sigismund] the crafts had been devised for this purpose that everybody by them should earn his daily bread, and nobody shall interfere with the craft of another.[4]

Jurisdiction has been a source of conflict among unions from the very origins of labor movements. It was the decisive schism between the Knights of Labor and the AFL, later between the AFL and CIO, and continues to be the major divisive element between the building trades unions and the industrial unions in the unified AFL-CIO.

The union situation following World War I made it patently clear that the craft-controlled AFL was incapable of establishing union power in the growing, mass-production sector of the American economy. Nor did the contemporary industrial unionists have a better record, but at least they expressed concern about the problem which the influential AFL circles dismissed as somehow ordained by a greater power.

The great turning in the history of union structure took place in the early and middle 1930's. The critical difference was the New Deal, the legislative enactments and general temper of which made mass industrial unionism feasible for the first time. John L. Lewis' genius consisted of the almost immediate perception of this new situation and the zeal to act with daring on this perception. Ultimately Lewis' perception, zeal, and, it should be added, money set in motion forces which led to the establishment of the Committee for Industrial Organization, and of industrial unionism as a going concern for both the CIO and the AFL.[5]

A union legitimates a claim to jurisdiction through one or more of three ways: through internal processes of the labor movement, through the procedures of a governmental regulatory agency, and through recognition by the employer in collective bargaining. The labor movement sanctions jurisdiction by means of a federation grant of jurisdiction to a national union, a national union grant to a local union, or the award of a judicial tribunal established under federation law. If the exclusive jurisdictional claim is subsequently confirmed by a government agency, it is most likely to be in a proceeding before the National Labor Relations Board.[6] Effective jurisdiction may be confirmed simply and most commonly by the employer's recognition of the union as the representative of his employees in a specific unit.

DIMENSIONS OF JURISDICTION

Union jurisdiction has four interdependent dimensions: (1) a description of the job or job groups; (2) the geographic area to which the work jurisdiction applies; (3) the specific purpose for which jurisdiction is being exercised; and (4) the level of union government to which the jurisdiction applies.

The job dimension of the jurisdictional claim is typically incorporated in a description of the workers covered, in terms of some combination of occupation, worksite, industry, employer, work process, materials, tools, and machinery. The classically succinct statement of job jurisdiction used to be that of the United Mine Workers:* "All workers employed in and around coal mines." The Airline Dispatchers claims simply "all aircraft dispatchers." [7] The Transport Workers' statement is in the same style of inclusive brevity: "All workers eligible for membership employed in, on, and about any and all passenger and other transportation facilities and public utilities in the United States, Canada, and possessions and territories of the United States." [8]

The Building Service job jurisdiction is expressed in terms of work, worksites, and occupations. Thus, work is identified as "maintenance, upkeep or servicing"; worksites as "all private and public buildings, streets and grounds, institutions, arenas, department stores, hotels and apartment hotels," and twenty-eight additional sites from cemeteries to dance halls; and occupations as "school custodians . . . and other non-academic school employees, porters, building washers, pin setters," for a total of more than one hundred separate occupations. [9] The IBEW jurisdiction is in part stated in terms of work process—"manufacture, assembling, construction, installation, or erection," and machinery—"equipment, apparatus, and appliances

---

* Most unions have such unwieldy names that in the body of the text either their common short forms or their initials will be used. Reference to the index will show that Miners or alternately UMW stands for the United Mine Workers of America; Carpenters for the United Brotherhood of Carpenters and Joiners of America, etc.

required in the production of electricity." [10] Occupation as "trade" is the basis of the Carpenters' job jurisdiction, which is claimed to be "all branches of the carpenter and joiner trade," enumerated as "carpenters and joiners, railroad carpenters, bench hands, stair-builders, millwrights," and twenty-five additional "trades." [11] A "materials" oriented job jurisdiction is illustrated by the Painters, who claim "all glassworkers, to wit, setters of art glass, prism glass, beveled glass, leaded glass, . . . all plastics or other similar materials when used in place of glass." [12]

Jurisdiction for entire industries or industry-groups is to be found in the Mine Workers as noted above, the UAW (farm, automobile, aircraft, and agricultural implements),[13] United Steelworkers (iron, steel, aluminum, non-ferrous metal),[14] AFSCME (state and local public service except, among others, teachers and fire fighters). Employer-based job jurisdiction is to be found in the unions of the various branches of the federal public service, as in the divisions of the postal service: Post Office Clerks (AFL-CIO) and Postal Supervisors (AFL-CIO), or the American Federation of Government Employees (AFL-CIO) for federal employees generally. In private employment, single-employer national (or at least interstate) unions are found in unions limited to employees of Westinghouse and Du Pont.[15]

The claims to jurisdiction which unions make in their constitutions, it must be emphasized, should not be taken at face value. For many unions, some part of the jurisdictional claim is hardly more than a statement of intent, hope, or insurance against a future contingency. "The only jurisdiction worthwhile," Woodruff Randolph, the long-time ITU president, once said, is "the jurisdiction you [can] get and hold." [16]

STRUCTURAL TYPES

No typology of union structure serves to convey the intricate variety in job jurisdictions, for jurisdiction in action is a function of practical problems. However, it is useful to classify unions according to three structural types. One is the "skilled" craft-trade-occupation-profession pattern, generally called craft unionism. Examples are Carpenters, Patternmakers, Fire Fighters, Airline Pilots, Actors, Musicians, Barbers, Typographers, and Railway Conductors. But craft, and therefore craft unionism, cannot be precisely defined. Helen Wood comes closest to providing a point of reference for a definition, by distinguishing between "vocational specialization among workers in occupations which require substantial amounts of specialized knowledge and skill and . . . the division of labor which stems from differentiated organization of work." On this basis craftsmen represent the former type of specialization.[17] There is also an institutional element in defining craft unionism. H. A. Turner has observed from his British experience that workers may be " 'skilled' or 'unskilled' according to whether or not entry to their occupations is deliberately restricted and not in the first place according to the nature of the occupation." [18] Or to put it another way, an occupation continues to maintain its standing as a craft because the union has been effective in protecting the perquisites of craft-like apprenticeship, restriction of worker entry, and the closed shop even after the specialized knowledge and skill associated with the craft have been reduced.

The characteristic craft union patterns are found on the building industry site with its distinctive crafts or trades (Bricklayers, Carpenters, Electricians, Iron Workers, Operating Engineers, Painters, Plasterers and Lathers, and Plumbers); in the railroads (Signalmen, Telegraphers, Trainmen, Yardmasters, Conductors, Patrolmen, Clerks, Engineers, Firemen, and Maintenance of Way); in the railroad shops (Machinists, Electrical Workers, Firemen and Oilers, Carmen, Sheet Metal Workers and Boilermakers); the printing trades (Typographers, Pressmen, Stereotypers, Photoengravers, Lithographers, Bookbinders, and Mailers); and in the maritime (Licensed Deck Officers, Licensed Engineers, Radio Operators, Pursers, and Unlicensed Personnel).

The second type is the semi-industrial, industrial, or multi-industrial pattern—meaning a jurisdiction in which all or almost all classes of workers at a given worksite or in an industry or in several industries are commonly included. The word industry as used here has no rigorous meaning. Craftsmen are included within many industrial jurisdictions, but most of the jobs "represent simple subdivisions of tasks rather than true differentiations by skill and required experience." [19]

Industrial and craft types of units are likely to co-exist in sub-units at all levels of union government. Important exceptions include the railroad crafts, the ITU, and the Patternmakers. One of the advantages of the intermediate body is that it permits the presence of both types under the same broad organizational umbrella at the same time that the "consciousness of kind" is retained in an identifiably separate suborganization, as will be shortly illustrated.

The federation as a type of organization has no distinctive structure, and consists of affiliated national unions of all structural types. When the AFL and the CIO existed separately, the AFL was generally predisposed to craft union interests and the CIO to industrial union interests.

The jurisdiction of a national union's subordinate bodies is pieced out as a result of unique circumstances. The work jurisdiction of the subordinate bodies is usually some segment of the national's. But it is not rare for a local's work jurisdiction to be outside of the formal jurisdiction of the national union and to take on a sporting mutation. For example, Local 12 of the UAW in Toledo, an "amalgamated" local, includes the employees of Buddies Box Lunch. The employees of the Xerox Corporation (a photocopy company) are in a Rochester local of the Amalgamated Clothing Workers. One-half of the plants organized by the locals of District 4 of the IUE were under the stated jurisdiction of IUE, eighteen in borderline jurisdictions, but thirty-seven clearly outside IUE's jurisdiction. "Anyone working under a light bulb," as some IUE union organizers quipped, was fair game.[20]

The International Ladies' Garment Workers' Union is a semi-industrial union type covering all production workers and truck drivers, except plant maintenance, and office workers. In New York City its critical levels of government are two intermediate bodies known as joint boards —a "dress" joint board covering the locals in the New York "market," and a "cloak" joint board (known formally as the Joint Board of Cloak, Suit-Shirt and Reefermakers'

Union of Greater New York)—representing the two major sectors of the industry. The locals comprising the Dress Joint Board each enroll members in the classes of work suggested by their names—respectively Cutters, Pressers, Italian Dressmakers, Dressmakers other than Italian. The Cloak Joint Board includes locals for each of the following: Operators, Finishers, Cutters, Shirtmakers, Pressers, Italian Cloakmakers, Button-Hole Makers, Examiners, Drivers.

The joint board is an intermediate governmental form which seeks to achieve unity in collective bargaining power at the same time that its constituent locals retain their distinctive jurisdictions (craft, trade, end-product, and language) for purposes of internal management and association. A craft local is "made up of workers who perform the same operations, as, for example, cutters or pressers or operators." A "trade" local in ILG usage includes "all workers making the same kind of garment, as, for example, neckwear workers, corsets, underwear, infants' clothes." An industrial local is "composed of all workers who make women's garments in a particular locality. They are organized in towns where there are not enough workers to make it desirable to organize by trades or crafts. . . . Language locals were set up only in the early days of the union for those who could not readily take part in union meetings conducted in any language other than their native tongue." [21]

The Iron Workers' national union claims as its jurisdiction "any bridge, structural, ornamental, shopman and re-enforced concrete iron worker, rigger, machinery mover, stone derrickman and pile driver." Apparently no local exercises a job jurisdiction as inclusive as the national union's. The jurisdictions of the locals fall into the following variations: (1) mixed—which includes all branches of the trade except shopmen and Navy Yard riggers; (2) shopmen; (3) structural, ornamental iron workers, riggers, and machinery workers; (4) shipyard riggers; (5) structural and ornamental; (6) re-enforced concrete iron workers; (7) Navy Yard riggers; (8) structural; (9) architectural and ornamental; (10) machinery movers, riggers and machinery erectors; (11) stone derrickmen.[22]

The Longshoremen (ILA) is an industrial union na-

tionally and at each port where it bargains, but the locals
are divided. At the New Orleans port, for example, they
are divided into "general longshore workers" with separate
locals for white and Negro workers, clerks and checkers
(white), dock loaders and unloaders of freight cars and
barges (Negro), sack-sewers, sweepers, waterboys, and
coopers (Negro), and banana handlers (separate Negro
and white locals).[23]

The geographic or spatial boundary of jurisdiction is
a function of the level of government in a given union. A
national (or international) union carries with it a jurisdiction for the United States and/or Canada. The spatial
boundaries of the local union range from a section of a
large city (as in the New York City construction crafts
and longshoring, and the Detroit auto workers) to a multi-
state territory (as in many locals of the Operating Engineers). The typical geographic scope of a local union is
compact enough to be serviced easily—which generally
means a city, county, or metropolitan area.

However, Local 542 of the Operating Engineers covers thirty-four counties in Pennsylvania, and the entire
state of Delaware.[24] Local 3 of the Operating Engineers
covers northern California, northern Nevada, Utah, and
the Hawaiian Islands.[25] Operating Engineers Local 139
includes the entire state of Wisconsin:[26]

> When a contractor employs operating engineers—
> particularly on heavy and highway work—he may
> require a large territory to find such projects and
> in which to keep expensive machinery in continual
> use. The factor of relative amount of continuing work
> in a locality operates on both the contractors and
> the workers.[27]

Local 459 of the IUE, although based in the New York
City metropolitan area, represents workers as far away as
Milwaukee, Chicago, and New Orleans.[28] The geographic
jurisdiction of the seagoing unions departs from the pattern
of most unions. There the basic unit of jurisdiction is the
port branch. Members have no permanent attachment to
a branch, but branch facilities in the major ports are
available wherever the member happens to be.[29]

The geography of intermediate body jurisdiction is

regulated by function and follows no fixed pattern. The bargaining-oriented district councils of the building trades unions tend to cover a labor market area. The bargaining corporation councils of the mass production unions cover a national territory. Many unions—railroad, Teamsters, Carpenters, Machinists—establish legislative councils over a state-wide area.[30]

STRUCTURE FOR COLLECTIVE BARGAINING REPRESENTATION

The contour of jurisdiction shifts with purpose or function. Collective bargaining is the union's function which has been most profoundly reshaped since the middle 1930's. The key factor in this alteration has been the regulation of collective bargaining by the federal government through the National Labor Relations Board, first under the Wagner Act (1935), and then under the Taft-Hartley Law (1947).[31]

The law requires employers subject to its jurisdiction to bargain exclusively with the duly constituted representatives of their employees in an appropriate unit [section 8a (5)]. This has pushed the unions to reshape their collective bargaining structure. The total impact of the NLRB has been to relocate the definition of jurisdictional authority from inside the labor movement to the federal government. The regulation of collective bargaining within the railroads and the airlines has not by and large had the same effect on their union structure, since the regulatory agency in this case, the National Mediation Board, has conformed its unit findings to customary union structures.[32]

The NLRB's unit determination becomes the ultimate test of legitimacy if a union's jurisdictional claim is to stand up in a contest either against the employer or against another union. Once the NLRB decides the unit, it confers an exclusive right to representation on the certified union [section 9(a)]. It establishes thereby what may be called a limited legal sovereignty for representation purposes on a particular union for a particular group of employees.[33] This sovereignty conferred on the certified union by the NLRB is not absolute, and is subject to challenge at designated intervals and under specified rules [section 9(e)(1)]. The challenge can come from a group which wants no union, or from rival unions. But, as long as the certification is operative, it acts as a bar against a displacement or replacement action.

The building trades preeminently represent the group of unions whose jurisdictional claims in contract construction have not been revised by the NLRB. This is because the NLRB has not been able to find a unit formula relevant and enforceable in a casual employment situation where the worker is not attached to a permanent employer but only to a labor market area within which he regularly changes employers.[34] The contrast here is with the NLRB role in factory union jurisdiction. "It is quite a different task to defend a unit on the picket line, with few limitations to employer opposition and rival unions, than to organize through quasi-political methods and to persuade an electorate to place an 'X' on a ballot." [35] The problems in getting an electorate to place an "X" on a ballot are underestimated, as Southern organizers have testified, but the central point is valid. Customary jurisdiction has in any case not been altogether excluded from the Board's consideration. "In making unit determination, the Board . . . has continued to give particular weight to any substantial bargaining history of the group," and customary jurisdiction just has not been controlling.[36]

The unit which is appropriate for union purposes in collective bargaining is in fact effectively appropriate for only some part of the purposes of collective bargaining. Thus the CIO, in petitioning for a particular unit, as Brown and Shultz observe, was immediately concerned with "structure for *organization* rather than structure for *bargaining*." [37] The outcome of the NLRB determination, Dunlop has said, is "an election district in which employees vote for or against representation by a labor organization." But in practice "the election district and the scope of the parties represented at the bargaining table [for negotiations] do not necessarily have any relationship to each other. The *true* bargaining unit is often not the election district." [38]

The employee's decision on representation—i.e., as to who shall represent a designated group of employees—only begins the process of collective bargaining. There still needs to follow collective bargaining negotiations to work out the terms of the agreement. Negotiation in turn leads into the administration or the enforcement of the agreement. Representation, negotiation, enforcement are each integral phases of the collective bargaining process.

The CWA basic "election district" or unit of representation is likely to be a department (plant or traffic, accounting or commercial) within a company (Southern Bell, Michigan Bell, etc.) in a particular locality. Negotiations are carried on, however, on a company-wide basis by a CWA district, and it is not inconceivable that broader understandings are negotiated between the A.T. & T. system-wide and the CWA national union. Day-to-day administration of the agreement is more likely to be within the jurisdiction of the representation unit, or of even fractional parts of the unit.[39]

In steel, the representation certifications were originally issued on a plant and even smaller basis. While there are hundreds of local unions and bargaining units for U.S. Steel, the major negotiations are carried on by the national union on a company-wide and, in recent years, on an industry-wide basis, for all practical purposes.[40] In the packinghouse industry the representation units in the multi-plant companies are on a single-plant basis, but the contracts are in the form of "single master agreements covering all plants organized by the union." [41] Managements of other multi-plant companies prefer the negotiation unit to be congruent to the representation unit as is characteristic in chemicals, oil, building materials, food, and baking.[42]

The pre-Wagner Act labor boards and the NLRB in its early years of the Wagner Act viewed the representation unit question from the standpoint of enhancing union organization. The AFL charged in fact that the NLRB was in favor of enhancing industrial union organization by its unit determinations. This was denied by the NLRB,[43] but, regardless of whether it had this bias, it may be concluded that in the long run the NLRB's sanction of larger-than-craft units to whatever degree provided a substantial counterweight to the traditional bias in favor of craft jurisdictions by custom and the AFL.

After 1937, the NLRB, subjected to intense pressures

from craft and some employer interests, receded from its "industrialism" and in effect made it easier to achieve craft severance from the inclusive units. The unit amendments to Taft-Hartley subsequently affirmed this greater leeway for separate units for the crafts and professionals. In addition, guards and custodial employees are now prohibited outright from joining a larger unit or from affiliating to a union which also admits non-custodial employees [section 9(b)]. Foremen and supervisors have been excluded altogether from the application of the law [section 2(3)].

In the 1940's, the craft unions began to take a rational view of structure and entered the NLRB lists with petitions for industrial units. The Machinists, Electrical Workers (IBEW), Boilermakers, Sheet Metal Workers, and Carpenters—all craft warriors in the battle over structure of the 1930's—have had no difficulty in adding substantial numbers of industrial units as a layer over their basic craft foundation. In the case of the Machinists, industrialism has perhaps supplanted craft unionism as its primary commitment.[44]

This industrialization of the craft national unions has not deterred them from also opting for craft units when a situation seems tactically to require it, or from giving vigorous support to the craft positions of the Building and Construction Trades Department in its debate with the Industrial Union Department of the AFL-CIO. Taking into account also the expansion of industrial union jurisdictions, the upshot has been a jurisdictional map composed of national unions with multi-industry jurisdiction and industry groups with multi-union representation.[45] A study by Neil Chamberlain based on 1953 data found: (1) "Five unions . . . [each] in more than forty industry groups"; (2) "Forty-three [unions] appear in ten or even fewer industries"; (3) the UAW had units in 36 industries, the Teamsters in 57 industries, and the Machinists in 51 industries; (4) almost half of the industries each "dealt with more than twenty different national unions." [46]

STRUCTURE FOR NEGOTIATION

The structure of units for representation determined by the National Labor Relations Board, as has been said, does not adequately portray structure for purposes of collective bargaining negotiations. The negotiation structure results from molding the representation unit into combinations "determined by the highly complicated interrelationships between the parties and by all kinds of market forces," as Dunlop says, and not from the choices of workers.[47] However, if the interrelationships stray too far from the choices of workers, it has not been uncommon in this period for the membership to force the return of negotiations—at least for a brief time—to the grass roots unit.

Most negotiation units are small, but there is a heavy concentration of workers for whom unions bargain (50%) in the larger units. Most employees—about two-thirds—are to be found in single-employer units. Multi-employer units "predominate in local product and service markets" while "single-employer bargaining predominates in national product and service markets." [48]

The negotiation jurisdiction may vary with different provisions of the same contract. The size of a wage increase and pension and insurance are the only provisions in a multi-plant corporation contract determined at the corporate and national union negotiation level. Invariably left to local option in multi-plant or multi-employer units are provisions relating to "(1) method of wage payment; (2) structure of occupational rates; and (3) seniority." [49]

The administration of the contract, especially in the earlier stages of the grievance machinery, is uniquely the one phase of collective bargaining which falls into local jurisdictions. In steel, for example, although negotiation is highly centralized "locals most certainly are masters of their own destiny in *living* under the contract." [50] But in railroads—another centralized negotiation situation—there are contralocal tendencies in grievance administration. Davey notes that "in many instances the requirements of a centralized bargaining relationship have virtually erased local autonomy in settling grievances," and attributes this to the "fear of setting up an embarrassing precedent." [51]

There is no clear-cut tendency in the size of the unit for negotiations and enforcement. The geographic expansion of particular markets acts to create a territory larger than can be looked after by one local union, and the local may typically be displaced in favor of an intermediate body. Local union control may also be displaced as a re-action to the coordination of manpower policies by a multi-plant corporation. Acting in a contrary direction to en-hance the relative power of local and sublocal units has been the militant assertion of rank-and-file job interests in the face of technological change, which is so much a part of the contemporary union climate. The rank and file's rebelliousness has been substantial enough to require re-negotiation of national understandings in order to make them acceptable to the local constituencies.[52] Decentrali-zation in the structure for negotiation has been accom-plished by the emergence of special forms for craft repre-sentation within some of the national industrial unions, largely as a reaction to the "skilled trades revolt" of the middle 1950's. These forms have developed such adapta-tions as local skilled trades committees, formalized repre-sentation in negotiations, and craft self-determination in approving contracts and in striking.[53]

TENDENCIES, IMPLICATIONS, AND THEORIES

It has been seen that the jurisdiction of any given union unit will vary according to the purposes for which jurisdiction is being defined. Hence the structural type which represents the best fit for a given jurisdiction will also vary with union purpose. A given union member can simultaneously be a member, and therefore subject to the jurisdiction, of (1) an industrial national union and a craft local union for purposes of internal self-government; (2) a multi-employer city-wide unit for purposes of con-tract negotiation; and (3) a plant unit for purposes of filing grievances. This is analogous to the individual citizen who is simultaneously under diverse public jurisdictions— federal, state, city, county, water district, educational dis-trict, park district, etc.—depending on the purpose for which jurisdiction is exercised.

The broad purposes for which jurisdiction is defined in the American labor movement are internal self-govern-ment and collective bargaining, with the latter frequently affirmed by an NLRB (or NMB) finding of appropriate unit for representation. The collective bargaining purpose is an aggregate covering many "subpurposes." Jurisdiction for representation does not always parallel negotiation or enforcement jurisdiction. The geography of jurisdiction for all purposes is, in the first instance, a function of the level of union government.

With the eruption of industrial unionism in the 1930's, something more happened than simply a modification of a structural form. Growing out of workers' needs in a mass production environment, industrial unionism brought with it—and was in fact part of—a larger complex of interdependent institutions and attitudes responsive to this mass production environment. Thus, in addition to being an inclusive structural form, industrial unionism is necessarily an elaborate system of government at the worksite, a relatively more powerful national union, a mass political movement, a new power center in the total society, an integrating force for masses of ethnic workers, a challenge to the quality of the industrial management performance, and a realignment of sectional interests within the labor movement.

Craft unionism—excluding the special case of the railroads—is also a product of a particular environment and it, too, has a style of behavior responsive to that environment. The influential elements in the craft union setting are a handicraft-like technology, a local product market, a casual labor market (for many crafts but not for all), and a simple mode of entrepreneurial organization. The effects of this setting on craft union government, as it touches the union member, have been to make the government in the union hall more important than the government at the worksite, the government of the local bodies more important than the government of the national, and the union business agent more important than any single employer.[54]

No one structural type dominates the labor movement in the way craft unionism did before 1933. Nor has the Webbs' seventy-five-year-old assessment materialized: "A Trade Union formed as it is, for the distinct purpose of obtaining concrete and definite material improvements in the conditions of its members' employment, cannot . . . safely extend . . . beyond the boundaries of a single occupation."[55]

The element of manual skill as a significant basis for

union jurisdiction is declining in importance, which helps explain why the ideal types of craft unions are on the wane in American unionism. Only the building trades craft unions continue undiminished in power; the long-established crafts on the railroads, in the printing trades, and in maritime are under great pressure from the sweep of technology. Craft skill claims continue to be made for jobs in NLRB representation hearings, but this is usually a tactical device for enhancing special interests.[56] In contrast, the skill or art of the professional continues to be a decisive factor in the marking out of sectional jurisdictions, as the entertainment talent guilds demonstrate. It is not unlikely that the resistance of the "new technology" professionals (engineers, etc.) to conventional unionism is in part due to a fear of loss of identity in unions that also cater to nonprofessionals—or to put it in terms of this discussion—an antipathy to unions that are "overinclusively" structured.

THEORIES OF UNION STRUCTURE

The controversy about union structure, from the inception of unionism, has involved more than the narrow question of which union form represents the most rational adaptation to the workers' job interests. Unionists and employers, reformers and revolutionaries, politicians, public administrators, and social philosophers, all have contributed to the historic running debate on the merits of inclusive versus exclusive forms of structure, or "craft versus industrial unionism."

The inclusive structural types were until recently regarded as more compatible with social reform and revolutionary objectives, and the narrower types with "pure and simple" trade unionism. As Robert Hoxie put it more than a half-century ago:

> Craft unions tend to be businesslike, selfish, non-idealistic, nonpolitical, nondemocratic; trades unions tend to be group-conscious and political; labor unions tend to be idealistic, moralistic, theoretical, political, but nondemocratic; industrial unions tend to be class-conscious, socialistic, and theoretical.[56a]

But Selig Perlman, writing in the same period, discerned that industrial unionism could be limited to job objectives and need not necessarily be a handmaiden of social up-lift.[57]

Craft unionism started out as a mode of practical ac-commodation, but later acquired an ideological coloration as a defense against the severe attack of the industrial unionists and the pro-industrial union intellectual. As an ideology, craft unionism offered its greater stability, sur-vival value, cohesiveness, bargaining power, and superior craftsmen's intelligence.[58] Since the 1930's industrial union-ism has on the whole lost its ideological aspects. "In the past," David J. Saposs observed early in 1935, "industrial unionism was primarily the hobby of the radicals. . . . [Now] some of the most influential conservative labor leaders are . . . strenuously championing industrial unions —at least for the integrated mass production industries." [59]

There is a kind of debate with implications for struc-ture now going on, but it is largely over conflicting job interests, as can be observed in the controversy over con-tracting-out by industrial establishments. The industrial unions are against contracting-out because it reduces the volume of work for their members. The building trades unions favor subcontracting because it increases the volume of work for their members. Managements appear to favor contracting-out as a simpler and more economical ad-ministration of the plant maintenance function. These kinds of interests are not fundamentally different from a juris-dictional dispute between two craft unions, although one suspects that something of the old ideological fervor gives the (building trades-industrial union) debate a sharper cutting edge. Union interests in jurisdiction are also in conflict in an NLRB craft severance context, that is, where a craft interest seeks to "sever" a "craft" unit from a more comprehensive unit.[60]

Employers' theories of union structure also grew out of ideology. In favoring the narrower units dividing craft from production workers, and in their dealings with rival unions of production workers in a multi-plant company, employers have applied the classic maxim of *divide et impera,* even though this made bargaining more difficult. Something like this maxim seems to be management strategy in the labor policies of General Electric and of the chemical, petroleum, and packinghouse industries. In each of these situations two or more rival unions are contending for power. Before the upheaval of the 1930's, managements were willing to incur the cost of dealing with the crafts as a way of avoiding the greater cost of dealing with industrial unions. The craft unions, moreover, seemed to offer no political challenge to employers as a class, whereas the industrial unions did.

The likelihood is that managements are now receding from this ideological position, and are judging the issue of structure from the viewpoint of economic efficiency. A case in point is the argument of the Manufacturing Chemists Association, a trade group which opposed severance in an NLRB proceeding because "of the extremely high degree of integration in the basic chemical industry." [61] The NAM has urged that "substantial weight should be given to the views of the employer based on the organization, management, and operation of the business from a functional, physical, and geographical standpoint." [62]

Throughout its history, the NLRB has had recourse to a variety of standpoints from which to judge the merits of the unit question: the enhancement of union organization, the stabilization of collective bargaining, the right of self-determination for craftsmen and professionals, and the conflict of interests (as in the question of a proper unit for confidential employees). The efficiency of the collective bargaining process has been only incidentally a standard for judging the appropriateness of a unit.[63] In exploring the relevance of union structure, or put another way, the implications of exclusive units versus inclusive units for the meaning of the larger values to be served, scholars have also set forth a variety of viewpoints and criteria: the preservation of workers' local self-government, the social balance essential to a pluralistic society, the efficiency of collective bargaining, the stability of the wage-price-productivity relationship, and the freedom of a free enterprise economy.[64]

Theories of structure, in summary then, have developed from a variety of standards, interests, and perspectives: (1) rationality—the relationship of structure to the efficiency of the enterprise and the full employment potential of the economy; (2) worker security—the relationship of structure to the worker's job interests; (3)

power—the relationship of structure to the relative strength of the parties; (4) ideology—the relationship of structure to a reconstruction of society; (5) democracy—the relationship of structure to the balance of "countervailing" forces.

CHAPTER III

The Local Union

The origins of American unionism, it is commonly agreed, are traceable to the point in economic development—at the turn of the eighteenth century—where "the separation of functions" between the employer and his men is clearly evident.[1] In the classic shoemakers theory of John R. Commons:

> It was the widening out of . . . markets with their lower levels of competition and quality, but without any changes in the instruments of production, that destroyed the primitive identity of master and journeyman cordwainers and split their community of interest into the modern alignment of employers' association and trade union. The struggle occurred, not as a result of changes in tools or methods of production, but directly as a result of changes in markets. It was a struggle on the part of the merchant-employer to require the same *minimum quality* of work for each of the markets, but lower rates of wages on work destined for the wider and lower markets. It was a struggle on the part of the journeymen to require the same *minimum wage* on work destined

for each market, but with the option of a higher wage for a higher market. The conflict came over the wage and quality of work destined for the widest, lowest and newest market.[2]

When employers sought to accommodate their labor costs to these market pressures by hiring green hands and paying less than the established minimum wage, the class of skilled mechanics who were especially threatened by these "competitive menaces" responded by forming the first unions, in the Webbs' sense of a "continuous association of wage earners for the purpose of maintaining or improving the conditions of their working lives."[3] "The personnel of the early continuous societies" in the United States, according to David J. Saposs, "was entirely that of handicraftsmen or skilled mechanics."[4] The first unions formed were "purely local in scope" and were organized to avoid competition between individual workers.

The first thing the early union leaders did was to write constitutions for their organizations. If the 1805 constitution of the Journeymen Cordwainers of the City of New York is a fair sample, the governing documents were "well-written and carefully thought out." It started out with the preamble, "to guard against the intrigues or artifices that may at any time be used by our employers to reduce our wages lower than we deem an adequate reward for our labor."[5] Other provisions prescribed the officers (president, secretary, and three trustees), the manner of their election, and their authority to preserve "regularity and decorum" at the local meeting by fining recalcitrant members (up to 6¢) who failed to keep "silent." Initiation fee was set at 43½¢ and monthly dues at 6¼¢. What amounts to a "closed shop" enforced by a concerted refusal to work with non-members was established in this early document. Fines were to be levied for failure to attend meetings and for the failure by a traveling journeyman to notify a local of his presence in its territory. The procedure for amending the constitution required proposal at one meeting and approval by two-thirds of the members present at the next meeting.[6]

LOCAL UNION CONSTITUTIONALISM

The constitution of today's local union is not fundamentally different. It is in the first place a "constitution," or more typically a "constitution and by-laws," covering the same areas, but in greater detail and more elaborately.

The typical constitution falls short of authorizing everything the union does, and this is largely due to the union officers' approach that if something is not expressly forbidden it may properly be undertaken. Since the passage of the Labor-Management Reporting and Disclosure Act of 1959,[7] union officers are more likely to be aware of the need for proper authorization for their acts in the constitution or in the minutes of a union body, in the event of litigation. Local unions belonging to a few national unions are subject to model constitutions and by-laws promulgated by their national union.[8]

The main features of local union constitutions may be represented by the following depiction of the range of matters about which they are generally concerned. One of these, of course, is membership.[9] The worker is admitted to union membership by the local union, and in order to qualify for admission he must be employed at a craft or in an industry coming under the union's jurisdiction. Additional requirements include American citizenship, "good moral character," and approval by two-thirds or a majority of those voting at a union meeting. A minimum age and a period of apprenticeship and/or work experience in the trade are prescribed for admission to craft unions. Almost all constitutions deny membership to members of subversive organizations usually styled as communist or fascist, or of "dual" or rival unions. Less commonly, supervisors are expressly disqualified from membership. Retention of membership requires "good standing" which is generally defined as not more than three months in arrears in the payment of dues or other financial obligations.

All constitutions specify the grounds on which the union may proceed against a member. These are suggested in Table I—a tabulation of offenses specified in the constitutions of 152 national unions.

TABLE I.

Prevalence of Selected Offenses Punishable Under
National and International Union Constitutions,
Early 1961

OFFENSES	NUMBER OF UNIONS
All constitutions providing grounds	152
General grounds	152
Violation of the constitution	114
Conduct unbecoming a member	42
Bringing disrepute on the union	15
Financial	85
Misappropriation	56
Fraud	28
Job discipline	99
Violation of collective agreement	54
Violation of work rules	47
Injuring fellow workers	31
Union loyalty	124
Dual unionism	41
Secession	46
Strikebreaking	37
Disclosure of union secrets	26
Subversive activity or support	43
Failure to exhaust internal remedies	64
Electioneering	66
Distribution of unauthorized or slanderous material	60
Falsifying ballots	9
Moral	37
Drunkenness	16
Felony	4

SOURCE: U.S. Dept. of Labor, Bureau of Labor Statistics, Bull. No. 1350, *Disciplinary Powers and Procedures in Union Constitutions* (Washington: G.P.O., 1963), p. 28.

Members can be disciplined by a summary procedure, that is by allowing "the imposition of punishment without a hearing or trial." [10] "Due process" in the union disciplinary procedure commonly begins with the filing of written charges by a member, and the serving of charges and of notice of hearing on the accused. The hearing is characteristically conducted by the local executive board or, less typically, by a specially designated trial committee. The accused commonly has the right to examine and cross-examine witnesses, to submit evidence, and to be represented by professional or nonprofessional counsel. The decision on the charges is rendered by the trial body and then submitted for discussion and review to the membership meeting. A right of appeal is always provided, and is submitted in some instances to an intermediate body, but more characteristically to the national president and/or national executive and the national convention in that order. Four unions—the UAW, the Upholsterers, the Marine Engineers Beneficial Association, and the Packinghouse Workers—provide a final line of appeal to an independent judicial tribunal.[11] Prescribed penalties can include reprimand, suspension, fines, expulsion, ineligibility for office, loss of membership, debarment from future membership, and loss of employment.

LMRDA enforces an internal union "due process" applicable to all disciplinary actions against members, except non-payment of financial obligations [section 101(a)(5)].[12] Its mandatory requirements include "written specific charges," a reasonable time to prepare defense, and "a full and fair hearing." But even before LMRDA, common law provided a basis for court intervention in the union disciplinary process; so much so, in the opinion of Archibald Cox,[13] that "the LMRDA adds little to existing law." [14]

For most local unions the membership meeting is the supreme authority. In locals with very large memberships, a delegate body takes the place of the membership meeting as the highest authority. Membership meetings approve the admission of new members, act as the last local resort on disciplinary actions, review financial administration, especially changes in the financial obligations of members (this is required by LMRDA [section 101(a)(3)(A)]), discuss proposed collective bargaining terms, and ultimately approve or reject the collective bargaining agreement, approve the calling of strikes, and pass on amendments to the local union constitution and by-laws. The monthly meeting is most common, and special meetings may be called if specified requirements are met. Majority vote governs for most enactments other than amendments to the constitution and by-laws, expenditures in excess of a specified maximum, assessments, fines, death benefits, and expulsions which often require an extraordinary majority.

UNION OFFICERS

Local union constitutions also govern the eligibility, election, and terms of officers. The local-wide officers—usually president, vice-president, financial secretary, recording secretary, trustees, and, in craft locals, the business agent—are elected by the membership (now required by LMRDA [section 401(b)]). Officers must be members in good standing for some stated time, usually a year, prior to nomination and must be, in the case of craft unions, employed at the trade. A substantial number of craft-type locals bar employers, apprentices, and supervisors from holding union office.

Candidates must be nominated at one meeting and elected at a subsequent meeting (LMRDA requires a fifteen-day notice for these meetings [section 401(e)]). Officers serve for a specified term, most commonly two years, although one year is not unusual, and three- and four-year terms have been set in a few instances. The LMRDA now limits the term for local officers to a maximum of three years [section 401(b)]. Election is by secret ballot. The frequency of the secret ballot provision has increased since its incorporation into LMRDA [section 401(b)]. The votes are counted by tellers normally appointed by an officer. Election safeguards other than secret ballot are unusual but are becoming more frequent since standards of campaigning and elections are also covered by LMRDA [section 401(c)(e)]. The LMRDA's election safeguards give bona fide candidates equal rights to union office facilities and entitle them to membership lists, observers at polls and at ballot counting [section 401(c)]. In addition, the law requires enumeration and publication of votes by the local and the preservation of ballots for one year [section 401(e)].

Executive boards consist of the constitutional local-wide officers and, as often as not, additional members at large from the membership or from specified constituencies within the local. The executive board meets twice a month or weekly, reporting to the membership meeting where its actions are subject to formal approval.

The salaries of officers are stated in specific dollar amounts or the constitution prescribes a formula for their determination. Part-time salaries usually fall within a twenty-five to fifty dollars a month range. The formula for determining remuneration usually aims at reimbursing the officer for time lost on union business and the remission of union dues plus a nominal sum on the order of $5 to $10 a month. All local union officers are subject to discipline and the general procedure prescribed for the individual member is applicable except that the LMRDA standards do not extend to officers.

The financial administration of the local union is regulated in great detail. Commonly specified are initiation fees (mostly $25 and under), monthly dues (typically from $3 to $5), reinstatement fees, and assessments. Local union constitutions limit the purposes for which assessments may be levied and frequently require their ratification by an extraordinary majority. LMRDA requires that all increases in dues and other financial obligations be approved by a majority secret-ballot vote after due notice. Typical dues reported in 1960 were from $3 to $4 monthly, typical initiation fees at $10 or less, and a small number of local unions set transfer fees on the order of $1.[15]

Authorized disbursements commonly include per capita payments to the national union and to other bodies to which the local is affiliated, death benefits, floral tributes, and unemployment benefits; and a small number of unions provide for strike or defense funds. Craft unions have more elaborate benefit provisions and their dues are higher, therefore, than industrial unions. A substantial number of locals prescribe auditing and reporting procedures and membership approval for disbursements over a stated amount.

"Conflict of interest" transactions by union officers must be reported and are illegal under LMRDA's fiduciary clauses [section 202, 501]. These transactions as exposed by the McClellan Committee had been of two sorts: profiting from participation in union business transactions, or profiting from "silent partnership" in the business of an employer with whom the union bargains. Even before the enactment of LMRDA "all union officers and employees" were "subject to the usual common law fiduciary duties of an agent," which was "seldom enforced." [16] LMRDA simply incorporates these common law duties in a statutory requirement. In addition, it makes embezzlement of union funds a federal crime [section 501].[17]

LOCAL UNION GOVERNMENT IN ACTION

Just as there is more to civil government than can be found in written constitutions and statutes, so there is more to the government of local unions than is contained in constitutional documents.

Collective bargaining is sparsely treated in local union constitutions. Occasionally constitutions describe the composition of the bargaining committee which is likely to be either the executive board plus additional members, or the one or two top officers. Most constitutions require membership approval of the negotiated contract by referendum or in union meeting. Many require a two-thirds vote of approval. The act of striking requires approval by the membership, usually by a two-thirds majority vote in secret ballot. Local union constitutions do not usually require—even where mentioned—the degree of accountability by the executive bodies that in fact prevails in handling grievances, formulating bargaining demands, reporting on negotiations, and calling strikes.[18]

The main thrust of racial or other discrimination with respect to membership does not stem from constitutions but from custom. Only two national unions (the unaffiliated Order of Railway Conductors and the Brotherhood of Locomotive Engineers) excluded Negroes by formal constitutional provision before the practice was made illegal by the Civil Rights Act of 1964.[19]

The locus of discrimination is the craft unions and particularly the railroad and building trades unions. The severe contraction of employment in the railroads probably makes the situation there almost hopeless. Within the building trades unions the discrimination is centered in the local union, recurring most persistently in the locals of the International Brotherhood of Electrical Workers and the Plumbers.[20]

Negro workers find it difficult to be admitted to craft unions because they are unable to find a sponsor or because apprenticeship opportunities are not available. Sometimes there are tacit agreements within the union to vote against admission of Negroes. Occasionally the local craft examination has been manipulated in order to fail Negro applicants. Inside the union, informal discrimination is not confined to the crafts and may take the form of segregation in separate or "auxiliary" locals, segregation of seniority rosters to restrict promotion opportunities, racial wage differentials, and racial imbalance in the makeup of the leadership corps.

While discriminatory practices have been reduced, they have not been eliminated. Gains on this front have been brought about by improvement in the economic situation, increased efforts of the labor movement to curb discrimination, the pressures of the Negro trade unionists within the labor movement and the National Association for the Advancement of Colored People outside the movement, and the strengthening of the legal position against discrimination culminating in the enactment of the Civil Rights law. While labor movement spokesmen claim that there has been a significant reduction in discrimination, civil rights leaders hold that very little change has taken place.[21]

It is too early to tell how effective the Civil Rights Act will be in curbing discrimination. The trade union section of the law makes it illegal:

(1) To exclude or to expel from its membership, or otherwise to discriminate against, any individual because of his race, color, religion, sex, or national

origin; (2) to limit, segregate, or classify its membership, or to classify or fail or refuse to refer for employment any individual, in any way which would deprive or tend to deprive any individual of employment opportunities, or would limit such employment opportunities or otherwise adversely affect his status as an employee or as an applicant for employment, because of such individual's race, color, religion, sex, or national origin; or (3) to cause or attempt to cause an employer to discriminate against an individual in violation of this section.[22]

Explicit restrictions on admission of members are now rarely incorporated in constitutions. The closed-shop-hiring-hall unions are in a position to make restriction of entry into the union equivalent to restriction of entry into employment. Where union membership is not a condition for hiring—which is the overwhelmingly prevailing condition—then there is no point in the union restricting membership.

Restrictions do exist in fact, however, but to what extent is hard to measure. The chances are that the practice of closing membership rolls outright is rare. Probably not as rare is the restriction on entrance into apprenticeship status or the limiting of apprenticeship to sons of members. High employment levels in the construction industry may be keeping this classic form of restriction to a minimum. Restriction by high initiation fees must also be rare judging by the paucity of cases which have arisen under the Taft-Hartley provision [8(b)(5)] which makes this an unfair labor practice.

Short of outright restriction, there is the practice of segregating workers by category, as in the West Coast longshore industry, where class "A" members have full membership and class "B" members are subject to bumping if not enough jobs are available for the first category.[23] A comparable institution is the "permit man" who is granted a temporary right to work, for a fee, but who is denied the full status of union membership.[24] The "permit man" or his equivalent is conceived as a kind of reserve labor force to meet seasonal employment peaks, and his second-class status is usually justified on this ground by the craft unionists. There are cases, however, where the permit practice is extended beyond this purpose so that it becomes a source of additional income for the local union treasury or a device to restrict voting rights of members.

The permit type of restriction, if it is part of a closed shop system, is probably illegal under the Taft-Hartley Law [section 8(a)(3)], and, if it is a device for restricting voting rights, is probably illegal under LMRDA [section 401(e)]. However, the practice has not yet been effectively prohibited. This is part of the general weakness in enforcing the Taft-Hartley provisions against the closed shop. Neither common law nor LMRDA have been interpreted to protect workers who are denied admission to union membership altogether. It is the Civil Rights Act and state fair employment laws which protect workers against discrimination in admission to union membership on grounds of race.[25]

THE MEMBERSHIP MEETING[26]

Most local by-laws incorporate a standard agenda for the membership meeting which includes: the pledge to the flag; the roll call of officers, with absences or reasons for absence noted; new applications for membership, with the applicants taking the "obligation"; reading of communications, usually from labor and political organizations soliciting attendance at meetings, conventions, and dinners; and approval of disbursement item by item, usually payments for "lost time," supplies, hall rentals, "per capita," and salaries.

The most important part of the agenda is the report of the officers on grievances, negotiations, and jobs. Questions on these matters are likely to arise from the floor. Committee reports, such as those from the education committee or the social committee, and reports from delegates to various affiliated bodies are likely to pass with little comment. The standard agenda also provides for such usual items as unfinished business, new business, and "good and welfare."[27]

The routine meetings are attended by a very small

proportion of the membership, rarely beyond 5 percent, but somewhat higher if there is a fine for failure to attend. The regular attenders are the officers, the activists, the inevitable "character," and the lonely members who have no other place to go. Union members are absent from meetings because they are bored with their formal processes, with other people's personal problems on the job (which take up most of the time of the meeting), and with the "bickering and politics" which are likely to mark the gathering. All attempts to exhort and induce attendance and to attract members to meetings tend to fail. Craft locals get a higher attendance than industrial locals because the union meeting is the place where the craftsman keeps up with developments in his trade and keeps in good financial standing. The factory worker, on the other hand, gets to see most of his fellow workers on the job.

The "crisis" meeting (not unlikely a special meeting) brings out a large attendance—somewhere between 30 and 60 percent of the membership—and sharp partisanship in the floor debate. The "crisis" is likely to be the formulation of contract demands, or the approval of the contract, a dues increase, a strike vote, a contested union election, or perhaps the question of disaffiliation or secession.

The very largest locals do not run monthly membership meetings. General meetings, if held at all, are reserved for crisis occasions or for other forms of demonstration, and then the meeting serves as an audience for officers' reports rather than an instrument of government. The membership meeting for these large locals is effectively replaced by delegate assemblies as the supreme local body.

The local union leadership is generally in control of the meeting, but rarely is the control either so efficient or firm that dissenting views are not able to get a hearing. The problem of the local union meeting, as Leiserson observed, "is not so much a matter of getting full attendance . . . as it is of making sure that free speech is guaranteed. One outspoken critic is often enough to hold officials to account and to prevent them from abusing their power." [28]

LEADERSHIP—THE BUSINESS AGENT[29]

Local union leadership can be classified according to whether it is local-wide or sectional, and whether it is part-time or full-time. Sectional leaders, of whom stewards are the most important, are part-time or volunteer. The most typical full-time, local-wide union leader is the business agent commonly found in the craft, non-factory, multi-employer local union.

The building trades business agent is the prototype. He is invariably the most important officer in the local. He is the chief bargainer and employment agency. He protects his local's jurisdiction against rival claims and polices the worksites to see that only union members in good standing are employed and union conditions are complied with.

The business agent's job protection function extends beyond his local union into the local labor movement. In the building trades council, and the district council of his own union he conceives as his most important responsibility getting a fair share of the available jobs for his constituents. And this is what they expect of him, too. The building trades business agent is actively engaged in the central labor body and the state federation because building trades unions have important stakes in legislation on occupational licensing, wage standards, and public construction. He is likely to spend time lobbying with the city council and the state legislature in behalf of and usually jointly with employer-contractors in his branch of the industry.

The typical building trades business agent is a man of power in relation to his union constituents who depend on him for their jobs, his contractors for whom his employment decisions are matters of economic survival, and the business agents of rival crafts with whom he is engaged in a running contest over jurisdictional claims. In this jurisdictional contest, the men who act more decisively and swiftly survive, because once a job is surrendered to another craft it is not likely ever to be recovered.

The business agent's self-view is that of a middleman mediating the struggle between the particularistic interests of his constituents and the economic survival needs of his contractors. Business agents tend to view the critical part of their jobs as keeping a "difficult bunch" in line,[30] "selling my men on the best deal," [31] or holding down "a lot of hotheads." [32] It is typical for him to think that "a union business agent can't be a business agent if he has a one-sided view—the union isn't always right." [33] The members of the building trades local judge the business agent's fitness to retain his office by his effectiveness in protecting the jobs in the local's jurisdiction, and his fairness in allocating the jobs among the members.

All local union leaders have to attend to the vital job interests of their members in order to stay in office. Within this constraint, the styles of union leadership range widely. There are a few of the bold, creative, "charismatic" types who have raised themselves above political rivalry within their locals. Harry Van Arsdale[34] of Local 3 of the IBEW, Harold Gibbons[35] of Local 688 of the Teamsters Union, and Joe DeSilva[36] of the Los Angeles Retail Clerks are of this type. These are men who also loom large in the total labor movement. They do not ignore the "bread and butter" interests of their members, but their collective bargaining and internal union administration have a flair and color. These men are in restless search for new worlds to conquer, and they are likely to embark on projects in education, medical care, and labor politics which win public attention for their unions and themselves.

There is the type of business agent who rules by the sheer force and drive of his personality. Michael Quill was president of the national Transport Workers' Union but his base of power was as the head of the local Transport Workers' Union. Quill's "humor, audacity, and blarney," as a reporter once put it, epitomized his highly charged style of union leadership.[37] Not all business agents are strong types. In the smaller locals it is common to find the business agent who is continually fearful of prospective rivals and who survives as part of a leadership alliance or in the shadow of a strong man.

There is a predisposition to racketeering in business agent situations which derives from the necessarily great power which the business agent exercises in the allocation of jobs in seasonal industries and the enforcement of labor standards in industries in which employment costs are a critically high proportion of total cost. The racketeering may take the form of kickbacks by union members to the business agent in return for preferential treatment in job assignments as happened in the much-publicized case of the longshoremen on the East Coast. It may also take the form of collusion between the business agent and employers in allowing deviations from the contract's labor standards in return for a bribe.[38]

LEADERSHIP IN THE FACTORY[39]

The part-time, local-wide leadership consists of the executive officers—the president, the secretary-treasurer— who customarily earn their livelihood from the enterprise in which they are employed rather than from the union. These part-time officers are hardly ever as effective as the full-time business agent because they lack the latter's opportunity to become familiar with conditions in the trade and with the local membership.

It is not usual to find local-wide leaders of the business agent type in the factory local. Where there is a paid full-time officer—and this is unusual except in the largest locals—he is typically an administrator of internal local affairs. The primary employment of the factory local-wide union leader is characteristically in the enterprise which also employs his constituents. When he receives pay, it is commonly either for time lost from his primary employment or for union work after hours. The local union leader in the factory exercises power on a more limited scale because, working at his job as he does, he is under the constant scrutiny of his fellows and of his management. He tends to exercise less power in relation to his management which is likely to be large scale, specialized, and bureaucratized. Temperamentally, the factory local-wide leader is less of a middleman and more of a rank and filer.

There are departures from type. A factory environment combined with a small scale enterprise and/or atomized market—the garment or job metalworking industries— produces business agent types who, like the building trades prototype, exercise considerable power over their employers' labor standards.

The bargaining committee, rather than any single leader, is usually the decisive influence in the factory, especially where bargaining is on a one-plant-company basis. The bargaining committee's responsibility also is likely to include representation in the grievance machinery, especially at the higher stages.

The factory environment, with its structured shop society and specialized management, tends to inhibit the exercise of strong individual power.[40] The non-factory environment by contrast—using the building trades again as a model—consists of small units of employees who rarely work at a site long enough to build up cohesion. Management in the non-factory situation is very simply organized. There is neither worker nor management power to counter a power-minded business agent effectively.

The local union is the least formalized of governments in the union system because much of its business is carried on face-to-face. By the same token, it is at the level of the local and the shop that the union has the most concrete meaning for the average member.

CHAPTER IV

The Local Union Substructure
and the Union Member

Almost every local consists of a substructure of smaller units. The main purpose of these sublocal units is to provide a viable organizational channel between the local union and the individual member at the workplace. The sublocal unit, in contrast to the local, usually lacks some attribute of a self-contained government in that it does not have authority to tax, discipline, or enter into a formal agreement with management.

The substructure of the non-factory local in the building trades, printing trades, retail, and wholesale trades is invariably "multicellular"; that is, the local's constituency is divided among several sublocal units reflecting the several workplaces where members are employed under contract. The factory local is more likely to be "unicellular"; that is, the factory local constituency is found at one main workplace. However, if the one workplace is large enough, it will have a substructure of its own which will be reflected in the union structure, as will be noted later.[1] "Amalgamated" locals—as the multi-shop locals are called in the UAW—combining several factory work-places are, however, not uncommon.

In a large factory the sublocal units are based on the division of employees by building and/or department, and by shift. Non-factory organization is usually simpler and, therefore, the union substructure is simpler. Construction sites, printing shops, and retail stores ordinarily have fewer layers of management authority than a factory workplace and, consequently, there are fewer layers of union authority.

The governmental forms which these substructures take can be conceived of "as embodying not one but two distinct governments," as has been observed, "each performing a different function for which an appropriate structure has been erected." [2] One system is part of the internal government of the local union as an organic unit; the other constitutes part of a bilateral system with management based on the collective bargaining relationship. These systems may be called the internal union substructure and the bargaining structure respectively.

INTERNAL UNION SUBSTRUCTURE

The internal substructure is most intricately devised in locals with a large or widely-dispersed membership. For example, Local 65 of the Wholesale and Retail Workers in New York City has 32,000 members employed by 2,000 employers:

> The Local . . . is subdivided into four major Regions solely for administrative purposes, each under a vice-president, and each Region in turn contains four to twelve sublocal unions, referred to as Units. Each Unit represents workers in a specific trade, such as paper-box workers; or in a craft, such as office workers; or attached to a major employer, such as "Beautyaid Cosmetics." The Regions represent more or less consistent and rational groupings of these Units, but the membership and their employers are too diverse to permit of any very broad grouping of likes. The rationale for grouping Units by Regions is trades not geography. Altogether, [the local] is

made up of forty-two Units with membership varying from 150 to 1,500.

Members are grouped not only by Regions and Units but by "crews." A crew is made up of 25 persons or less, who elect their steward. Some crews include members from more than one shop, as is the case with office workers in small establishments; other crews may be made up of all or some of the employees of an employer. Crews meet on call either of the steward or of the organizer.[3]

Local 6 of the Hotel and Restaurant Workers with 25,000 members, to cite another example, is divided into geographic districts which in turn subdivide into shops. An annual general assembly, which is more like a convention than a union meeting, is the supreme legislative body. The executive power is vested in an executive board of seventy members elected by the membership.

Local 3 of the IBEW in New York City, with 33,000 members, is divided into two major sections. These are subdivided into twenty-two separate divisions, each of which has its own subgovernment, one of which, Division I, actually runs the local. Local 32 B of the Building Service Employees, also in New York City, has 40,000 members, and bargains with 2,600 employers. It is divided into seven geographic districts. The chief legislative instrument is three local-wide union meetings annually.

The 8,400 members of Local 3 of the American Newspaper Guild are divided into fifty employer units. The membership meets at the unit level, not at the local-wide level. For local-wide government, a representative assembly composed of three hundred delegates meets monthly. Transport Workers Union Local 100, comprising the employees of the municipally-owned subways in New York City, is divided into seventy-eight sections:[4]

The conduct of union affairs in the shop need not always be formalized into a government, especially if the local-wide leadership sees the shop leaders as potential rivals. This seems to be the case in Local 65 of the Wholesale and Retail Workers where Mrs. Cook notes "the officers want an unobstructed organizational relationship."[5] Shop organizations exist in Local 6 of the Hotel and Restaurant Workers but "whether they have any organic relationship to the governing bodies of the union . . . is doubtful." [6]

BARGAINING SUBSTRUCTURE

Closest to the worker's interests is the shop government established for collective bargaining, or the local's bargaining substructure. The conception of collective bargaining as a system of government goes back to the nineteenth century, at least as far as Webbs' *Industrial Democracy* (1897).[7] John R. Commons and several of his students represented collective bargaining as "industrial government," and a 1920 account of the pioneering collective bargaining relationship between the Amalgamated Clothing Workers and Hart, Schaffner, and Marx was titled by one of his students, "Due Process of Law." Malcolm Sharp—who wrote that account as part of a series of articles on *Industrial Government*—characterized James Mullenbach, the umpire under the agreement, as "a judge in a court of original jurisdiction," dispensing justice for the workers—"the republic of eight thousand people." The agreement "was the constitution of the republic" and the negotiators "a legislative assembly of union and company representatives meeting every three years." [8] Another student of Commons', Sumner Slichter, gave wide acceptability to collective bargaining as a system of "industrial jurisprudence . . . introducing civil rights into industry . . . requiring that management be conducted by rule rather than by arbitrary decision." [9]

Professor Hoxie described the stages of the collective bargaining process as analogous to the legislative, judicial, and executive functions of a government, respectively: "(1) the creation of a trade agreement, (2) the interpretation of the agreement, and (3) the enforcement of the agreement." [10] To apply Hoxie's parallel further, the constitution of the shop-centered industrial government may be represented as the collective agreement negotiated by the union and the management. The analogy to a constitution is more than superficial, for the written agreement is a kind of "higher law" [11] negotiated at established intervals and amended by special stipulation. The grievance procedure representing the enforcement branch, as it were, is rule-making on a case-by-case basis.[12]

The grievance procedure is an expression of the need for a mechanism to apply the agreement to the day-to-day problems in the shop. A few union agreements permit management to file grievances. In many establishments the grievance procedure is also available for any complaint which an employee may have about his conditions of work and employment whether or not these are contract-related.

The situations which induce the most grievances are, from the "griever's" standpoint, wrongful disciplining by management, improper job classification, and improper application of seniority to layoff or promotion, roughly in that order. The outcome of the grievance process is binding on the parties during the life of the agreement; the whole point being that the grievance procedure is the union's equitable alternative to direct-action methods like the strike.

The formal grievance process is incorporated in the agreement and specifies the number of steps between the presentation of the grievance and final determination.[13] The non-factory procedures are simple. If the foreman or supervisor is not able to settle the employee's complaint, the steward, or more likely the business agent, tries to adjust it. If it is not adjusted, the complaint is settled by arbitration which is resorted to only in a very small fraction of cases.

The factory procedures are likely to be more elaborate and prescribe a sequence of three or four steps beginning with the worker's presentation to his supervisor with or without the presence of a union representative. If this fails, then successive appeals run to either a steward-supervisor or an "international representative" step, or local bargaining committee-plant superintendent step, and the whole process is topped by impartial arbitration. A three-step procedure is illustrated by the Ohio Brass Company and IAM agreement:[14]

STEP	FOR EMPLOYEE	FOR COMPANY
1	Employee and/or departmental steward	Foreman
2	Shop committee	Factory manager or representative of the personnel department
3	Officer(s) of the union or authorized representative(s)	President of the company

A six-step procedure is illustrated by the agreement between Rohm and Haas Company and the Glass Workers:[15]

STEP	FOR EMPLOYEE	FOR COMPANY
1	Employee	Immediate supervisor
2	Shop steward	Immediate supervisor
3	Area grievance man	Departmental foreman
4	President of local union or his representative	Personnel director
	JOINT INDUSTRIAL RELATIONS COMMITTEE—NOT MORE THAN:	
5	Seven union representatives	Seven management representatives
6	Seven union representatives, but must include president of international union or his representative	Seven management representatives, but must include manager of industrial relations

Under some union regulations, the local executive board or the union meeting must approve arbitration in view of the substantial outlay for smaller locals which arbitration is likely to entail. A contract may exclude some issues from arbitration and, in that event, if the parties cannot agree on their own, the union is free to strike.

THE STEWARD

Grievance committeemen are usually compensated by the management on a time-lost-from-work basis. For this reason, contract or practice regulates the number of grievance representatives, their districts, and the maximum lost time allowable for reimbursement. The average number of employees per steward is not known, but it may be on the order of 100 to 1. The steward is supposed to be elected by his constituency, but the job is not always highly regarded and it is not uncommon for the local union officers to coopt the most available worker into stewardship.

In some locals the steward body is part of the governmental system of the local union, functioning as an executive board or bargaining committee. In addition, to pay for lost time, the steward is likely to command such union perquisites as dues remission or a nominal fee contingent on attendance at steward membership meetings. The most important job perquisite is "superseniority," existing only in a minority of contracts, which gives the steward the right to be the last man laid off. The rationale for this is that only if the steward himself has maximum job security can he represent his constituents without fear of jeopardizing his own position as an employee.

The steward is subject to continual exhortation by his union. He is told how indispensable he is to the union—"the best contract in the world is worthless unless it is enforced by the steward" or "the steward is the communications link between the union and the rank and file." He is exhorted in the union's steward manual to know the contract, to distinguish between "a gripe and a grievance," to get the facts before he acts, to keep a record of all grievances, to be prudent and calm in his dealings with management, to settle grievances at the first level, to avoid horsetrading, to accentuate the positive, and not to disagree with his fellow workers in front of management.[16]

Unlike his European counterpart, the American steward is not a center of dissent against either the paid leadership or the management. In the American system of collective bargaining, he is a part of the union which is the exclusive representative for the unit. If the steward is critical of anybody, it is of the passiveness of the average member "who lets management walk all over him" without complaining.[17]

Although he is constantly urged in the more socially aware unions to educate his constituents in political action and legislative issues, the steward's paramount concern is how to cope with his constituents and his opposite number in management. It is the steward who experiences the full impact of potential tension and conflict in the shop: men versus women; crafts versus production; day shift versus night shift; age versus youth; whites versus Negroes; ethnic group versus ethnic group; incentive worker versus day worker; and, of course, workers versus foreman. He encounters, in short, all elements of difference in interest which may emerge among people in their personal relationships at work.

Not only diversity in interests but conflict arising out of personality differences is the lot of the steward. In this connection the steward is likely to single out "troublemakers" and "radicals"—that is to say, persistent grievers—the weak-kneed, the powerless, or the overbearing foreman in the management camp. He meets problems which have nothing to do with bargaining, such as poor materials, car pools, blood banks, workmen's compensation, and lovers and sweethearts, all of which get to him simply because he is there.[18]

The steward takes a flexible view of the meaning of the agreement. Thus, it has been found in a detailed observation of four factory situations that "prior to formalizing a grievance by writing, the steward initiates several extra-legal . . . contractual steps. Side agreements," or understandings between stewards and foremen, "either violate the written terms of the agreement or deviate from general practice in the shop." But these "understandings" work better than the contractual processes.[19] Another study observes the same kind of extralegal flexibility in "fractional bargaining," whereby strategically situated work groups are able to make private grievance settlements exceeding and, therefore, in effect renegotiating a provision of the agreement.[20]

The regular meeting of stewards is a common feature

of shop government. The meeting functions as a clearing house of grievances, a "downward" line of communications for the local-wide leadership to "disseminate information on bargaining progress," and an "upward" line to advise on bargaining strategy. The minutes of one stewards' meeting of less than two hours duration show that the following varied matters were discussed: the piling up of grievances; the job security concerns of the employees prompted by reduction-in-force rumors; "a hazardous working condition"; a report on the settlement of a long-standing grievance regarding misclassification; confirmation of a rumor that 2,000,000 caps were returned because of "bad lithography"; a complaint "that company puts on Kerr line workers with no experience and expects the same production." [21]

In the general run of factory situations there is no doubt that "the steward is an important person in the union's grievance machinery." [22] In the non-factory situation, especially in construction trades and service employment, the steward is a minor actor in the enforcement machinery. This may be due to the fact that the local unions in these types of employment usually use business agents whose presence tends to reduce the steward to a kind of "answering service." By contrast, the union shop group in the typical factory does not have as ready access to a local business agent. The union representative who comes closest to the business agent in the factory situation is the "international" or "district" representative who services a much larger territory than the local and who is, moreover, appointed rather than elected. In these circumstances the stewards must rely more on their own power.

Regular and special membership meetings as part of the governmental process of the sublocal groups are common but not universal. For example, both the ITU and the UAW explicitly authorize the holding of such meetings.[23] "Shop meetings are invariably better attended than local meetings," it has been observed, "because they are closer to the membership [and are] one of the most important institutions of self-government." [24] The shop meeting is closer to the membership in a physical sense and is likely to be held on or near the plant premises immediately after work, or in the case of the second and third shifts, immediately before work. In one such reported meeting the following problems were aired from the floor by the membership: "take-home" pay; "what can we do about getting our just bonus"; "they put me in a class-6 job and I am only class-3." [25]

GOVERNMENT AND SOCIETY

Government in the local substructure differs in several important respects from that in the local union. First, the sublocal unit is rarely a "complete" government, usually lacking the taxing, contractual, and disciplinary power of the local. Second, the grievance system is a bilateral government in which the union and the management participate jointly: The grievance system functions almost always in response to some prior, allegedly wrongful act of management. Third, the constituents whom the union must represent in the grievance handling are by law all employees in the unit irrespective of union membership—although the pervasiveness of union security provisions has reduced the force of this distinction. Fourth, a given sublocal unit is part of a complex of other employee units in the workplace with diverse national union attachments. This is true, obviously, at the craft-structured workplaces in railroads, printing, maritime, and construction. It is also true in varying degrees in many factory establishments. Fifth, the local union has the capabilities of representing not only the member's general employee interests in a labor market, but also his political interests as a citizen. The sublocal unit is almost totally restricted to representing the employee in the narrow job-employer context.

An appreciation of the number and character of units which might be found at a large factory workplace can be gained by imagining that all the employees eligible for unionization did elect the full variety of possible "appropriate" units available to them under existing law. This would result in the following array of units: a production unit represented by an "industrial" union; a series of separate maintenance units divided into several crafts—electricians, painters, machinists, etc.—each represented by separate unions; a shop clerical unit, i.e., clerical employees in the tool room or requisition depot; an "office" clerical unit, i.e., the white collar clericals in the front office represented by an office workers union; a series of separate technical and professional units—draftsmen, engineers and time-study men; a truck drivers unit.[26]

The participation of the union member in the affairs of his plant union is not limited to the formal governmental processes of unionism or of collective bargaining. The factory as a workplace organizes the workers and management into a society. The union member is consequently also a part of what has been variously styled as an "informal organization," "shop society," and a social system based in the plant. William F. Whyte speaks of "the factory [as] . . . a social system having its own equilibrium conditions." [27] The shop society complements union processes. Thus, it has been observed that "Members who do not attend meetings hear in the shop about what happened at the meeting from those who were there." [28] The shop society also provides a convenient and compact area for the organizing of group interests within the plant, and within the union in the plant.[29]

Cohesiveness of the shop society and the strength of union identification vary widely. To the extent that the external larger community is at some remove from the shop, "the union becomes a kind of working-class party, or even government for these employees, rather than just another association among many." [30] Miners, the operating railroad workers, longshoremen, sailors, and loggers "form isolated masses, almost a 'race apart.' " [31] For construction and maritime workers the shop society is the "union hall" society, especially in the hiring-hall industries where the members congregate waiting for job orders from employers. Factory work groups differ, it has been suggested, depending on their place in the technological system. "The social system erected by the technological process is . . . a basic and continuing determinant of work-group attitudes and actions." [32]

THE UNION MEMBER

What the worker expects from his job shapes what he expects from his union.[33] The worker wants economic security, by which he means a stable level of employment, a wage compatible with his workplace status and with an acceptable standard of living. He wants his job to be satisfying, by which he means some personal control over his own work, work pace, and work method. The worker wants equitable treatment in the workplace, which means for him protection against arbitrary management action. He wants to be consulted about changes in his situation, and he wants to be able to gripe without fear of reprisal. Finally, the worker wants to be part of a congenial work community, which means for him a pleasant place to work and good fellows to work with.[34]

In general, the worker's outlook tends to be short run, particularistic, pessimistic, and defensive. Even in periods of high level employment, insecurity is an ever-present element in his assessment of the future. His situation is never quite so good, he feels, that it cannot quickly change for the worse. "So far as the workers are concerned," Professor Hoxie pointed out, "there is no society as a whole, and no long run, but immediate need and rival social groups." [35] The typical trade union member is a "business unionist," and he wants his union to be a "business union, stressing," in Selig Perlman's classic formulation, " 'shop rights,' which, to the workingman at the bench, are identical with 'liberty' itself—since, thanks to them, he has no need to kowtow to foreman or boss, as the price of holding his job." [36]

Most members believe they belong to a democratic union, meaning that the union is governed by the wishes of the majority. Members are critical of their officers' performance, but think they are doing as good a job as can be expected. Most union members have no great ambition to be union leaders, and are likely to lack confidence in their educational qualifications and ability to talk back to the employer—an attribute which they value highly.

The union which has concrete meaning for the member is the local union. As the level of union governments gets more remote from his direct experience, it diminishes in importance. Political and legislative activity by the union has the support of the rank and file member, but he wants union interests in politics to be closely linked with job economics.

This composite profile of union member attitudes and interests is, of course, subject to qualification. Thus, the union is more important to male members than to female members. The attachment to a particular union is greater among craftsmen than among production workers. The creative and artistic professional, especially in the entertainment field, puts great store by the union, which functions like a guild. The scientific professional feels remote from the conventional union of which he is a member.

CHAPTER V

The Intermediate Body
in Union Government

A feature of union government is the intermediate body which is a federated association of local unions. It represents a consciously rational effort to adapt organization to function by remedying defects in the organizational relationship among locals, or between locals and the national union. It serves to minimize rivalry and to enhance the effectiveness of the local unions over some common area of interest.[1] The intermediate body may take many different governmental forms and serve a variety of functions, as Table II indicates.

The intermediate body is utilized most commonly by a group of locals to achieve a common objective in collective bargaining.

Multi-local collective bargaining interests in a city, county, metropolitan, or local labor market area are enforced through intermediate bodies known by such various names as the joint council in the Teamsters, Building Service Employees, and Hotel Workers; the joint board in the ILGWU and ACWA; the district council in the Carpenters, the Iron Workers, and the Hod Carriers; and the district lodge in the Machinists. Intermediate bodies for local

TABLE II.

Intermediate Structure Classified by Type

I. DISTRICT OR JOINT COUNCILS—COMMUNITY-BASED—DELEGATE BODY

Union	Intermediate body	Primary function	Formation*	Local affiliation†
Teamsters	Joint councils	Supervisory	Mandatory	Mandatory
Carpenters	District councils	Bargaining	Mandatory	Mandatory
Iron Workers	District councils	Bargaining	Mandatory	Mandatory
Hod Carriers	District councils	Bargaining	By G.E.B.	Mandatory

* Formation

Mandatory: constitution requires they be formed by locals themselves when certain conditions exist.

By G.E.B. (General Executive Board): constitution requires they be formed by international executive board rather than locals themselves.

By Int'l. President: constitution requires formation by international president.

Voluntary: formation is at option of local unions.

N.M.: not mentioned in constitution.

† Local affiliation

Mandatory: constitution requires all locals in area (or industry, or company) affiliate once intermediate body has been established.

Voluntary: affiliation is at option of locals.

Union	Intermediate body	Primary function	Chief officer	How chosen
Building Service Employees	Joint councils	Service	Mandatory	Mandatory
Hotel Workers	Joint executive boards	Bargaining	Mandatory	Mandatory
Laundry Workers	Joint councils (state-wide)	Consultative	Voluntary	Mandatory
State, County and Municipal Employees	Councils	Service	Voluntary	Mandatory
Newspaper Guild	District councils	Consultative	Voluntary	Voluntary
Retail Clerks	District or joint councils	Consultative	Voluntary	Mandatory
Longshoremen	District councils	Legislative	Voluntary	N.M.
Clothing Workers (ACWA)	Joint boards	Service	By G.E.B.	Mandatory
Machinists	District lodges	Service	By G.E.B.	Mandatory

II. REGION OR DISTRICT—ADMINISTRATIVE ARM OF INTERNATIONAL UNION

Union	Intermediate body	Primary function	Chief officer‡	How chosen§
Operating Engineers	Regional offices	Service	Reg. Director	Pres. appoints

‡ Chief officer
§ How chosen

Pres. Appoints: appointed by international president.
E.B.M. (Executive Board Member, ex-officio): international.
Conv. Elects: elected at national convention usually by caucus delegates from region or district.
Int'l. Officers App't.: appointed by the four officers of the international union.
Members Elect: elected by members in district by ballot.

Union	Intermediate body	Primary function	Chief officer	How chosen
Communication Workers	Districts	Bargaining	Dist. Director, E.B.M.	Conv. elects
Electrical Workers (IBEW)	Districts	Service	Dist. Vice-Pres.	Conv. elects
State, County and Municipal Employees	Regional offices	Service	Reg. Director	Pres. appoints
Retail Clerks	Divisions	Service (organizing)	Org. Director	Pres. appoints
Longshoremen (ILWU)	Regional offices	Service	Reg. Director	Int'l. officers appoint
Steelworkers	Districts	Service	Dist. Director, E.B.M.	Members elect
Auto Workers	Regions	Service	Reg. Director, E.B.M.	Conv. elects
Machinists	Territories	Service	Vice-President, E.B.M.	Conv. elects

III. INDUSTRY OR COMPANY COUNCIL OR CONFERENCE—DELEGATE BODY

Union	Intermediate body	Primary function	Formation	Local affiliation
Teamsters	National trade divisions	Consultative	N.M.	N.M.
Newspaper Guild	Chain councils	Consultative	Voluntary	N.M.
Electrical Workers	Councils	Bargaining or	Voluntary and	

Union	Intermediate body	Primary function	Formation	Local affiliation
Railroad Trainmen	Gen. grievance committees	Bargaining and grievances	Mandatory	Mandatory
Railway Clerks	System boards of adjustment	Bargaining and grievances	Mandatory	Mandatory
Railroad Conductors	Gen. committees of adjustment	Bargaining and grievances	Mandatory	Mandatory
Auto Workers	Corp. & industry councils	Bargaining	By G.E.B.	Mandatory
Machinists	District lodges (in Aircraft, Air Transport, Railroads)	Bargaining	By G.E.B.	Mandatory

IV. STATE COUNCILS AND CONFERENCES—LEGISLATIVE ARM—DELEGATE BODY

Union	Intermediate body	Primary function	Formation	Local affiliation
Teamsters	State conferences	Legislative	Voluntary	Mandatory
Carpenters	State councils	Legislative	Voluntary	Mandatory
Hotel Workers	State councils	Legislative	Mandatory	Mandatory
Electrical Workers	State associations	Legislative	N.M.	N.M.
Railroad Trainmen	Legislative boards	Legislative	Voluntary	N.M.

Union	Intermediate body	Primary function	Formation	Local affiliation
Railway Clerks	Legislative committees	Legislative	Voluntary	Mandatory
Railroad Conductors	Legislative committees	Legislative	Voluntary	N.M.
Steelworkers	Legislative committees	Legislative	N.M.	N.M.
Machinists	State councils	Legislative	Voluntary	Voluntary

v. AREA CONFERENCES—FOR EXCHANGE OF INFORMATION—DELEGATE BODY

Union	Intermediate body	Primary function	Formation	Local affiliation
Teamsters	Conferences	Consultative (service)	By G.E.B.	Mandatory
Operating Engineers	Conferences	Consultative	N.M.	N.M.
Laundry Workers	Conferences	Consultative	N.M.	N.M.
Office Employees	Conferences	Organizing	By G.E.B.	Mandatory
Machinists	Conferences	Consultative	Voluntary	Voluntary
State, County and Municipal Employees	Conferences	Consultative	By Int'l. Pres.	N.M.

VI. OCCUPATIONAL SUBDIVISIONS—COUNCILS AND DEPARTMENTS

Union	Intermediate body	Primary function
Longshoremen	Caucuses	Consultative
Auto Workers	Skilled trade councils	Bargaining
	Skilled trade department	Service (for bargaining units)
Steelworkers	Salaried office and technical workers dep't.	Organizing and service
Machinists	National Tool and Die Conference	Consultative
Iron Workers	Shop department	Service

SOURCE: L. A. O'Donnell, "An Inquiry Into Union Structure—The Intermediate Body," unpublished Ph.D. thesis, University of Wisconsin, 1961.

joint bargaining can be composed of locals of diverse national unions, as, for example, the Hotel Trades Council, which includes not only locals of the Hotel and Restaurant Workers but also locals of the IBEW, Operating Engineers, Firemen and Oilers, Building Service, Painters, Upholsterers, and Office Employees.[2]

An intermediate body can function as the bargaining arm of an international union in a multi-state area. This is so with the "regional office" in the Operating Engineers and the Longshoremen, the "territory" in the Machinists, the "district" in the Communications Workers and the IBEW, the "division" in the Retail Clerks, and the "region" in the Auto Workers. This kind of regional intermediate body is likely to develop from the top down—that is from the national union to the locals—and is a means for reducing the administrative distance between the national union and the locals.

The intermediate body becomes national in scope when it undertakes to coordinate multi-local bargaining interests with one employer or industry within the national union. These types of intermediate bodies are variously styled: "national trade division" (i.e., bakery, dairy) in the Teamsters; "chain councils" (i.e., Scripps Howard) in the Newspaper Guild; "general grievance committees" (by railroad) in the railroad unions; "corporation councils" (i.e., GM or Agricultural Implement) in the Auto Workers; and "conference boards" (i.e., Westinghouse) in the International Union of Electrical Workers.

There are also occupationally-based intermediate bodies, which cover a national territory. Examples are in the Skilled Trades Conference of the Automobile Workers, the White Collar and Professional Conference of the International Union of Electrical Workers, and the Salaried Office and Technical Workers Department of the Steelworkers. This form of intermediate body is, in many respects, a pressure group within the national union. It reflects and re-enforces a sense of group identity and seeks to prevent the submergence of its special interests within the larger national union.

FUNCTIONS OF INTERMEDIATE BODIES

One of the critical facts about intermediate bodies is the extent to which they displace local union authority in collective bargaining. The clearinghouse type of intermediate body does not go beyond exchange of information, as, for example, with the "joint councils" in the Laundry Workers and Retail Clerks, and the "area conferences" in the Operating Engineers and the Machinists. However, there are also the intermediate bodies with greater authority which achieve binding action by specific consent, as in the "corporation councils" of the UAW and the IUE.

A service type of intermediate body is exemplified in the "regions" or "districts" of the industrial unions like Auto, Steel, and CWA. International representatives attached to these regions or districts primarily service the constituent locals in the negotiation of contracts and the handling of particular grievances. The local union in this relationship to the district is commonly free to accept or reject the assistance of the international representative. Finally, there are the intermediate bodies with complete authority over collective bargaining—the district councils of the Carpenters, and the joint boards of the needle trades unions. In this relationship the local unions have been completely displaced in the making of collective bargaining and strike decisions.

Intermediate bodies designed to achieve political purposes also exercise differing degrees of authority. The multi-local legislative interests within a national union in a state are organized through a representative state council. The continuous involvement of the railroad unions in legislation makes the state legislative body a very important element in the governmental pattern of these unions. The state legislative council is also found in the Teamsters, Carpenters, Hotel Workers, and the Machinists, among others.

GOVERNMENT

The local's obligation to affiliate to an intermediate body may be compulsory, voluntary, or contingent. Thus, the local may be compelled to join with others in forming an intermediate body when prescribed conditions exist—for example, when there are two or more locals in a given area, the local may exercise the option of affiliating with an intermediate body; or such affiliation may be contingent on order of the national executive board or president.

Except for the intermediate body which is a "regional" or "district" administrative arm of the national union, policy making is exercised by a body of delegates elected by the constituent locals. The local district or joint council types of intermediate bodies meet regularly throughout the year for the transaction of business. The others also meet regularly but less frequently. The bargaining type of industry or company council is primarily active at the time of contract negotiation.

The power exercised by the intermediate body leader turns, of course, on the power which in the first instance is exercised by the intermediate body as an organization. Those bodies with effective authority over the constituent units tend to produce strong leaders. The strong executives are apt to be found in the "regions," "districts," and "territories" of the industrial unions (IAM, UAW, USA, CWA, IUE). The district or regional director in these unions is invariably a member of the national's executive board, and manages a staff of "international" representatives whom he hires or who are hired on his recommendation. The same is true of the city-wide joint boards in the needle trades. Although there is provision for a delegate joint board, the joint board manager is the main source of power. The intermediate bodies of the administrative type in the craft unions (i.e., regional offices of the Operating Engineers, the districts of the IBEW), have no significant authority over the locals.

The corporation council of the UAW and the IUE is structurally a delegate body, and is able to make its power felt on the director.[3] The general committee in the railroad unions (as in the Brotherhood of Railroad Trainmen) is in a similar position in relationship to its full-time chairman who is a full-time officer.

The executive officer of the intermediate body is designated variously: (1) by appointment of the national union president or national executive body, as in the case of the Teamsters' conference director and the Amalgamated Clothing Workers' joint board manager (until Landrum-Griffin); (2) by election at large in referendum, as in the case of the IAM vice-presidents, but subject to presidential assignment as to territory; (3) by election in convention caucuses of the appropriate local union delegates, as in the case of UAW's and CWA's district directors; (4) by membership referendum in the district, as in the case of Steelworkers' district director; (5) by election of the delegate body, as in the case of Teamsters' joint councils and the general committees of the BRT.

DETERMINANTS OF CHARACTERISTICS

The elaborateness or simplicity of intermediate body organization is not so much a function of size as of kind and number of union problems. The Steelworkers union with one million or so workers is simply structured, probably because the founders, Lewis and Murray, were opposed to the creation of potentially contentious subbodies.[4] Only the geographic district intervenes between the international and the local. The Teamsters and the UAW, by way of contrast, are elaborately structured. The UAW intermediate structure is a network of industry councils, corporation councils, and occupational councils, and regions reflecting UAW's administrative sophistication, pressures from below for representation, and diversity of membership interests. The Teamsters union is structured nationally into trade divisions; geographically into area conferences subdivided into area trade divisions; and finally into the joint councils. Some of the UAW elements are also present in the Teamsters, but the main factor has been the push of the union's recent presidents for centralized power in an historically decentralized union.

The West Coast Longshoremen, with a membership of less than 100,000, has three types of intermediate bodies: district councils, which are "almost exclusively oriented to political action"; regions, which are administrative branches of the international; and caucuses, which are mechanisms for debates over collective bargaining problems.[5] The Railway Conductors, with a membership of 25,000, has a general committee of adjustment for each railroad system, an association of general chairmen, and a legislative committee in each of thirty-five states.[6]

Intermediate bodies are established to give some order to the haphazard nature of local union jurisdictions and to achieve a greater congruity between jurisdiction and the employers' market structure. The Central States Drivers Conference of the Teamsters has sought centralized collective bargaining over a multi-state area in order to compensate for the shifts in the employees' hiring base from high-wage areas to low-wage areas. The enlargement of the market area over which collective bargaining is integrated permits employers "to translate wage gains into higher prices with little loss of business." [7] The importance of the character of the market in shaping Teamster behavior can be seen from a letter written by Joseph Adelizzi, director of the Empire State Highway Transportation Association, to Teamster President Tobin in 1958:

> The situation today for both management and labor in our industry here is far from healthy, indeed, it might be termed critical. With so many Local Unions in the picture, all of them having the same and overlapping jurisdictions and many of them having different wage rates and conditions, stable competitive conditions are virtually impossible. This more or less intolerable situation is such as to make contract enforcement difficult if not impossible.[8]

The joint boards of the needle trades unions negotiate and enforce their contracts in the chief branches of the industry within major clothing market areas so as to control the work bundle from manufacturer to subcontractor. The employer and industry councils in the steel, auto, rubber, and electrical manufacturing unions bring the local unions into an intermediate body capable of standardizing wage rates and other employment conditions over an area as wide as the industry's or employer's domestic operations.

Intermediate bodies are formed to permit the pooling of staff resources in negotiating and enforcing the contract, and to service local unions which could not meet the demands put upon them, if left to their own resources. This can now be seen in insurance and pension administration, where the advantages of risk pooling and a broader membership base lower administrative costs and improve the quality of service.[9]

The resources of several local unions banded together in an intermediate body provide a more viable base for experimentation and aggressive leadership. Many of the men of power, influence, and creativity in the needle trades unions derived their effectiveness from the broader scope of activities allowed in a joint board. The programs of these unions in education, arbitration, and industry stability could not have been undertaken by small local unions.

Intermediate bodies in the Steelworkers, Machinists, IUE, Teamsters, and AFSCME have been used at various times as bases from which to mount—as it turned out—successful campaigns against national union presidents. But the intermediate body in the service of a determined national union leadership can also act to consolidate national union power. This seems to be the way in which President Hoffa has been using the area conferences and drivers councils in the Teamsters—not, however, without resistance from local unions.[10]

The intermediate body has its uses in mediating sectional grievances against the national union. It provides a mechanism through which sectional interests and groupings can function within the national union rather than take the form of a secession movement. The most striking examples of this are the skilled trades councils in a number of the industrial unions. Conversely, in unions with predominantly craft interests intermediate bodies may provide organization for the expression of factory workers' industrial interests. The Lumber and Sawmill Workers in the Carpenters unions, with their own district councils, is a case in point. The failure of the pulp and paper unions to consolidate their West Coast locals resulted in a massive secession movement and the organization of a new union.[11]

No inexorable logic is at work to bring about the formation of intermediate bodies. The Steelworkers do not use intermediate bodies such as the corporation council or the industry council as do the UAW or IUE. The growth of large corporate enterprises in the baking industry has not yet produced effective corporate-wide intermediate bodies in the bakery union, although this is approximated by "the same representatives of national firms and of the national union [moving] from city to city to engage in local bargaining." [12]

The precise structuring of intermediate bodies within a national union is thus shaped by many forces: size, diversity in worker constituencies and in market environments, the requirements of efficiency, political considerations, and still other factors.

CHAPTER VI

The National Union—
Constitution and Convention

The national union occupies the kingpin position in American trade union government because of its decisive influence in collective bargaining—the core function of American unions. Of all the elements in the union governmental system, only the national union is capable of functioning under its own power in the modern industrial environment. Local unions which are not part of national unions can function only in restricted areas, and the federation derives its influence and power from being an association of national unions.

As a generic form of union government, the national union evolved out of a series of institutional encounters, first with the forces of local union autonomy, then with the "politicalism" of the central labor body, and, finally, with the centralism of the federation.[1] The early local unions were at first reluctant to cede much of their effective authority to national unions. The central labor bodies saw their political and legislative goals diluted by the economic preoccupations of the national unions. Earlier national associations of unions, like the Knights of Labor, saw the brotherhood of man constricted by the materialism of the national trade union. Ultimately, none of these could stand up against the national union's superior adaptability to the dynamics of American industrial society.

When the CIO came into being, the central position of the national union was already established as a fundamental principle of American unionism. For a time, the towering role of John L. Lewis and the CIO in the formation of national unions after 1935 seemed to threaten this principle. But as the national unions shed their financial and organizational dependency on the CIO, they behaved in a traditional autonomous manner.

Jurisdictional conflict, civil rights practices, and racketeering in the national union have been subject to AFL-CIO intervention. But the federation has had to exercise its power with discretion and weigh its use against the limited tolerance of strong national unions which could always "disaffiliate." The national union continues to be unchallenged in its control over collective bargaining and routine internal administration even in the face of the enhanced authority claimed by the AFL-CIO in recent years.

Three major factors contributed to the ascendancy of the national union's focus on economic objectives and reliance on economic weapons over the claims of political action as a means to the solution of worker problems: (1) Market expansion exerted pressure on unions to construct forms of organization capable of functioning over a national job territory. "In the field of trade unionism," John B. Andrews noted, "the nationalization of the market gave birth to the national trade union." [2] (2) There were no later political aims comparable in their power to move the working class as universal manhood suffrage, a goal which was achieved relatively early. (3) The national union developed essential capabilities in financial administration and collective bargaining, and with these, the exercise of effective controls over local unions. It should be emphasized, of course, that the term "ascendancy" applied to the national union is relative, for prior to 1933 the national unions, effective as they were in surviving, never penetrated beyond the "backward" technological sectors of a fast-rising industrialism. Most of the industrial economy remained untouched by direct union organization.

According to the Bureau of Labor Statistics, most national unions have the distinguishing features of "collective bargaining agreements with different employers in more than one state" and in infra-structure of subordinate bodies, usually of the local union type.[3] While some of the maritime unions "have a unitary form of government" with no subordinate bodies, they are counted as national unions.[4] Unions of public service employees are frequently limited to one employer, but, though failing to meet the terms of its definition, in this regard unions of government employees are nevertheless classified as national unions by BLS. In addition, BLS automatically confers national union status on any AFL-CIO affiliate.[5]

On these bases, BLS counts 181 national and international unions with headquarters in the United States— 130 of which are AFL-CIO affiliates.[6] The ten largest unions, each with over 400,000 members, accounted for over 43 percent of total membership; 85 unions, each with fewer than 25,000 members, represented less than 4 percent of total membership.[7] In 1963, the national unions embraced a total of 73,587 local unions. The UAW has 1,271 locals; the Steelworkers, 3,100; the State, County, and Municipal Employees, 1,644; the Postal Clerks, 6,235; the Teamsters, 871; and the Carpenters, 2,100. At the other extreme are Aluminum Workers with 54 locals, Broadcast Employees with 57, Cigar Makers with 34, and American Communications Association with 6.

THE CONSTITUTION

The "fundamental" governing document of the national union is a constitution. The "fundamental" quality of union constitutions falls something short of being a higher law[8] because there is, for practical purposes, no "inferior" law. There is no class of union legislation which stands in the relationship of statutory law to constitutional law as in the civil government.

National union constitutions are adopted by a representative convention. Every ensuing periodic convention is nominally free to amend the constitution and is commonly referred to as a "constitutional" convention. It is rare for constitutional amendments as such to require approval at a higher union level. It is not uncommon to require membership approval through referenda for enactments on prescribed subjects such as dues increases, assessments, and election of officers.

The constitution of the national union has evolved to its present form in three phases. In the founding phase, the constitution served its classic purpose by limiting the powers of the central government. The early national unions were in effect local union compacts, and the founding locals were therefore careful to incorporate restrictions on the power of the national union. In both the United States and England, the early national unions were essentially federations of almost autonomous local unions. One object of their constitutions was to preserve the rights of the locals against the federated national union, except as a limited grant of power was expressly conferred.

As market and other circumstances compelled and enabled the national unions to enlarge their controls over the locals and to function in collective bargaining on their own power, the constitutions evolved further to transform the locals into subordinate bodies. The latter lost their original autonomy. Leiserson has observed:

> In the early years of the present century, the national unions perfected their internal government and administration, established adequate revenue systems, developed methods of making joint agreements with groups of employers, and extended their working rules into national laws. To safeguard the stability of the organizations and the collective relations with employers established by the agreements, they gave national officers more control over locals and disciplining of members, required national authorization or approval of strikes, and established strike benefit funds as a means of enforcing the controls.[9]

The national union constitution thus became a broad and somewhat indefinite outline of the governmental framework. As various students have pointed out, "The wording of the constitution is rarely precise and clear. Much of its meaning depends on knowledge of prevailing practices in the trade or industry to which it applies." [10] It is "a dubious guide" to jurisdiction.[11] The intermediate bodies "are sparsely described." [12] Failure to mention the local union substructure is not uncommon.[13] The specification of collective bargaining and strike procedures are defective when measured against what actually takes place.[14] The constitution, in most cases, tended to become a ritualistic document bearing little relationship to practice except, perhaps, as controversy or litigation forced it to acquire more realistic features.

In the third and present phase, the constitution begins to take on the character of a charter which authorizes the main union functions and, in a few instances, even affirmatively protects individual membership rights against the local union and the rights of the locals against the national union.[15] This perception of the constitution as a realistic document was in large part the product of the increasing number of legal actions brought against union officers for violating or exceeding constitutional authority.

LMRDA has established constitutional authorization as an explicit test of the legality of trusteeship, convention, elections, and financial administration [section 302, 401(b), 501(a)]. Under that statute, the obligation of fiduciary imposed on union officers requires them "to manage, invest, and expend" the money of the union "in accordance with its constitution and by-laws" [section 501(a)]. As a result of LMRDA, approximately three-fourths of the national unions amended their constitutions in respect to the conduct of local union elections and disciplinary powers and procedures. By 1962, thirty-four national unions had amended their trusteeship provisions.[16]

The accession to power of a rebel group may in the first stages provide for a move in the direction of constitutional union government—as in the case of the Association of Western Pulp and Paper Workers. The new constitution which it adopted contains a section on "Rights of Member—Due Process" guaranteeing "the right to participate in all decisions of the organization, . . . the right to run for office and to criticize organization policies and officers." [17] Earlier, the union publication had editorially advocated as "a further safeguard for permanent democracy . . . a fair and workable check and balance system among the officers and other groups having operational duties." [18] The rebel group recently come to power in the AFSCME has proposed a constitution which incorporates a bill of rights along the LMRDA model and an express separation among legislative, judicial, and executive powers.[19]

As a result of LMRDA, the national constitution is now closely scrutinized by the union's lawyers, and is likely to undergo further changes. Typically, it is not yet a document which expressly limits the power of the executive over members and subordinate bodies. A few constitutions —the Machinists' for example—assert that "all authority and power not specifically delegated to the officers in the constitution is reserved to the membership." [20] The emphasis is still on the affirmative powers of the executive and the responsibilities—rather than rights—of members and subordinate bodies, but important changes in this regard should be expected to occur. It has been observed that:

> The first members of the national unions were the delegates sent by the local unions to the national conventions. Other individual unionists were originally regarded as members of their respective local unions only. This early restriction of national citizenship reflected the original concept of the national union as a federation of local organizations which retained a considerable measure of sovereignty. The early national conventions were thus regarded as meetings at which the representatives of the virtually autonomous locals would enter into compacts for the mutual advantage of their respective constituencies. In some early unions, the national union was not considered to possess an existence independent of the convention of local representatives.

But the national union as an aggregate of convention delegates from local unions was not suited to the circumstances of the traveling union member who had no established local base. Consequently, the traveling members also had to become members of the national union. This development marked the beginning of the member's primary citizenship in the national rather than the local union.[21]

The subordination of the local union began with the superior services made possible by the larger resources of the national union, especially in respect to national strike benefits. These gave an "added value to membership in the federation" at the same time that they "increased international control over strikes." [22] It was only gradually that the national union became what it is today, holding "sovereign power . . . supreme over all members, local unions and other subordinate governing bodies." [23] The national union began as a creature of the locals. Today, the local union as an organization is almost always created by the national union[24]—and this isn't a recent tendency. Professor Hoxie reported on this development as early as 1915.

> While, historically speaking, the local is the parent body and the union fabric or organization is the result of integration, currently the growth of unionism is for the most part just the other way—from above downward. The internationals, in general, and the American Federation of Labor have each their paid organizers whose business is to go about the country among unorganized workers, preach to them the advantages of unionism, get them to apply for a charter, organize them, and teach them to run their union local. The local thus organized is a product of the international or national, chartered by it, largely directed by it, bound to obey it in matters of policy and method or suffer revocation of charter, [or] loss of counsel and financial support in time of trouble—all of which ordinarily means speedy dissolution.[25]

In the earlier 1900's, the referendum was in great vogue in American national unions, reflecting the widespread political movements, largely agrarian-based, for direct, popular government. In 1913, 95 out of 113 nationals were using the referendum, primarily "between the sessions of the convention to transact business which [could not] be wisely entrusted to the executive board, yet can be postponed only with grave inconvenience until the next convention." [26]

Only a minority of unions now use the referendum, and this in very limited ways, as the ultimate source of union authority. The election of national officers by referendum vote occurs in about one-fourth of the unions, accounting for about 30 percent of union membership.[27] The referendum does not seem to affect the frequency with which opposition candidates are elected to national union offices.[28]

The Machinists represents one of a few large unions in which the referendum is still utilized not only for the election of national officers but also for changes in the constitution, dues, and officers' salaries and pensions.[29] More typical is the experience of the Carpenters. Until 1957, "the referendum was the basic decision-making institution." [30] During that decade, referenda resulted in the rejection of some of the actions approved by previous conventions. In addition, they were costly, were participated in by only small proportions of the membership, and encouraged one-candidate elections. As a result, the referendum was displaced by the convention as the supreme authority of the national union.[31]

THE CONVENTION

Supremacy in the contemporary national union is vested in the convention. It is the instrument which mirrors the evolving nature of the national union. At first, as has been seen, the convention was the national union, for the latter was essentially a federation of local unions. Union membership ran to the local not to the national union—only the convention delegates were members of the national. When the business of the national union became so demanding that it could not wait for the convention, the national union began to acquire full-time paid officers, and equal representation of affiliates regardless of membership gave way to representation weighted by membership. Subsequently, the referendum emerged as a check on the convention, but then diminished in importance. Finally, the convention became the supreme governing body of the national union in effect, directed by its executive board. Today, the constitutional subordination of the local union is complete.

The convention, Leiserson observed, partakes of "the functions of a constitutional assembly, a legislature, a

supreme court . . . [and a] . . . nominating convention." [32] The routine union convention is also a pageant,
a reward for drudgery back home in the local union, and
an operation in public relations. Ideally, the convention is
the occasion when the national officers render a report on
their stewardship for review and judgment by the delegate
body. As a legislative body, the convention sets forth the
policy agenda for the ensuing period. The convention is
thus the voice of the rank and file holding the national
officers to account and mandating a program for the period
ahead.

There is, obviously, no perfect fit between what the
convention is in action and what it should be like ideally
as an instrument of union government. In most cases, however, the gap between the actual and the ideal is not
large. Thus, the report rendered by the executive body is,
in most unions, a detailed and comprehensive "documen-
tary history" (as the ACWA calls it) of the union's activities
since the last convention, going far beyond the accounting
which most other membership organizations make to their
constituents. Even before LMRDA, the financial report indicated how the union's money was generally spent—for
many unions in considerable detail.[33] Critics can voice their
objections before the convention or at committee meetings,
but at some conventions vigorous criticism is voiced with
peril. The delegates do weigh their votes on significant
issues with an eye to their effect upon their constituents.
On balance, the convention, conceding all its defects,
makes possible a more rational and democratic administration of the national union's affairs than was possible
under the referendum.

Constitutionally, the convention is an assembly of the
constituent locals with voting strength weighted according
to membership in good standing but not always propor-
tionately. There is a tendency to favor the smaller locals
in the weight attached to the vote and the number of
delegates allowed per unit of membership.[34] However, the
chances are that this advantage is offset by the fact that
smaller locals are less likely to send their full complement
of delegates, if they send delegates at all.[35] Most union
conventions are held biennially or annually. The over-
whelming majority of unions hold conventions at intervals

of four years or less.[36] LMRDA prescribes an interval not exceeding five years in duration [section 401(a)].

The convention commonly has the authority to amend the constitution without further submission to the membership. In the present period, it is rare for a convention to go by without the adoption of a constitutional amendment, largely in consequence of LMRDA compliance. Some unions, like the BRT, go through the entire constitution line by line at every convention.[37] Others, like the OCAW, make the debate over structure and government their main business.[38]

The convention legislates through formal resolution and approval of committee and officers reports on three classes of subject matter: (1) *Internal government:* most importantly dues and the division of authority as among the president, the executive board, and the subordinate bodies. (2) *Collective bargaining policies:* in some of the older craft unions the convention acts upon "laws" which are in effect conditions of employment that the subordinate unions must insist upon in bargaining; in the industrial unions the convention establishes broad bargaining priorities which are generally not binding in detail on actual negotiations. The intent of these bargaining resolutions is to create a mood, general direction, and strategic climate rather than a legal mandate. (3) *Resolutions in support of domestic and international public policies:* the industrial unions are more likely to pass resolutions on broad policy—the crafts unions on issues more immediately related to their job interest, although the latter is not ignored by the industrial unions. These resolutions are passed routinely except when an issue with immediate union impact comes up.

Convention controversy has arisen over civil rights resolutions in unions with organizing problems in the south, or a "free trade" resolution for a union affected by foreign competition. Earlier, international issues—Marshall Plan, "second front," isolation versus intervention—represented an ideological trial of strength and prestige between communist and anti-communist groups. The importance of the public policy resolutions, even when they are routinely passed, lies in the foundation which they lay for the union's ensuing political and legislative program.

The deliberative work of the convention takes place in committees. These are usually appointed by the president, but in a few unions they are designated by the executive board and in a few elected by the convention.[39] It is in the committee room rather than on the convention floor that the interaction of interests takes place. Heated debate and a trial of strength in the committee room precedes many resolutions that are passed matter-of-factly by the convention. Many committees—especially the credentials and resolutions committees—hold hearings prior to the convention. Most constitutions require that resolutions be submitted by constituent locals at a time prior to the convention.[40] A minority requires the issuance of a report to the convention accounting for the resolutions submitted and justifying recommendations. Actually most of the resolutions are drafted in the national union.

Committee assignments are allocated to reliable and influential delegates, providing an opportunity for the chairman or the secretary of the committee to address the convention. On issues where preciseness is important, union technicians are likely to have prepared preliminary drafts and later act as secretaries to the committees.

The most important judicial function of the convention is to sit as the union court of last resort on appeals from decisions of the president or the executive board.[41] The delegates decide the appeal on the basis of a report from an appeals committee, and the defendant is generally accorded time to argue his case before the convention. In a small number of unions (cwa and ocaw, for example) the right of convention appeal is extended to staff members.[42]

Four unions have established so-called "public review" boards as alternate routes of appeal from the decisions of the executive. The review boards are composed of public members who have no connection with the union and are designed to provide "the accused an opportunity to appeal to a body that [is] separate and free from control."[43] The jurisdiction of the uaw board covers discipline cases and cases involving violation of the afl-cio Ethical Practices Codes. The Upholsterers' Appeal Board may decide cases involving disciplinary actions against members and union employees. meba limits its National Panel to cases of impeachment of local and district elected officers. The Packinghouse Workers Commission has the authority "to do those things necessary to insure proper and effective administration of the affairs of the International Union." [44]

As an electoral body, the union convention in the large majority of cases nominates and elects the national union officers. In a small number of unions the convention nominates and the members elect.[45]

The convention is a mood as well as a function. As much as anything else the convention is pageantry and good fellowship. The convention hall is festively decorated. Presidents, governors, mayors, and cabinet officers troop up to the podium to attest to the greatness of the union and its leaders. For the local leadership, attendance at the convention is a reward for service faithfully rendered. The local union secretary who has been laboring in the union's vineyards gets away from the shop and the union hall and for a brief moment every two or three years finds relief from his daily tedium. The delegate's wife gets to learn something about her husband's work because she, too, is commonly included in the delegate's expenses. If a contest for office is in the wind, tension, excitement, and, once in a while, violence fill the convention floor and "smoke-filled rooms." The caucuses run to all hours of the night. Rumors of deals, of shifts in delegate commitments are the order of the day and night.

CHAPTER VII

The National Union—
Leadership and Administration

The circumstances out of which the national union evolved, as we have seen, favored a strong organization. It is understandable, therefore, that these same circumstances have tended to favor strong leadership and administration in the national union. The executive board, executive council, or board of directors, as it is variously called, is the main source of direction in the national union and, given no split in its ranks, is in most unions also substantially in control of the union. Leadership in the executive board begins with the president, who is, in effect, *primus inter pares*.

Executive board members are either elected at large or by a geographic constituency. If by the latter, the election is by a membership referendum in the region or a vote of the regional caucus of delegates at the convention.

The main administrative responsibility of the executive board member in most industrial unions is directing a regional intermediate organization of the kind described earlier (Chapter V). This is the pattern in steel, autos, and telephones. Members of executive boards elected at large may be assigned to a full-time territorial constituency by the president and/or the board, as in the case of IAM. In the older craft unions the executive board members are elected at large, but perform only nominal regional duties in behalf of the national union. This type of executive board member continues to function mainly as the head of a local union or intermediate body, as in the case of the Teamsters. Or the executive board may be composed of a combination of headquarters-based board members, i.e., an executive vice-president or resident vice-president and locally-based board members. This is found in the Meat Cutters, ACWA, and ILGWU.[1] There is the now rare rank and file executive board, as in OCAW, where the board members are required to be workers out of the fields and plants, the theory being that the full-time officers need to be checked by board members who are still working at their jobs.[2]

The degree of constitutional power exercised by national union presidents has been classified by Professor Philip Taft as "routine," "moderate," and "considerable." The presidents with "routine power" are essentially administrators of policies established by the executive board as a group. In the "moderate power" group are the presidents who "enjoy considerable power," but their exercise of this power is subject to approval by the executive board. The largest group of presidents are in the "considerable power" category. Power for the national union president consists of virtually unrestricted authority to regulate local affairs and to appoint national union representatives. Some of the very powerful can interpret or set aside the national union constitution as in the Teamsters and Musicians, and remove elected national union officers as in the IBEW.[3]

The rationale for vesting great power in the union executive is that the union is constantly in the middle of struggles with employers who, in political terms, are "absolute monarchs." The president must have the power, it is argued, so as to deploy the union's resources swiftly and decisively to match the strategic advantages available to the "absolute monarchs." The need for strong executive power is asserted even by the spokesman for a new union formed as a rebel protest against excessive executive power in the national union. "The constitution must recognize that the union's officers, particularly the president, must have the authority to direct those working for the AWPPW if the best interest of the members is to be served." [4]

Constitution or not, the circumstances in which most national unions find themselves encourage strong presidents. In the national union headquarters there is no offsetting power that in other large organizations is exerted by a "bureaucracy" or an executive body. Of the executive body, only the secretary-treasurer and an executive vice-president are usually on the national union premises. Only in the event of schism does the executive body function consistently as a countervailing power. There is some evidence, however, that the LMRDA is exerting some sort of countervailing influence.

Considering their memberships, the national headquarters organization of most unions, with the possible exception of the railroad unions, is very simple. The elaborateness of railroad union headquarters is accounted for by the importance of the insurance and legislative functions. Judged by their personnel, most national union headquarters are hardly more than bookkeeping operations. There is little of the elaborate administrative network one expects to find in organizations with several hundred thousand members, and very little of the checking and balancing of executive power which a bureaucratic network tends to exert.

There is little evidence to indicate that the internal audit by a union committee, or for that matter by professional accountants, has ever uncovered even the grossest misuse of funds. Such meager evidence as is available does suggest that LMRDA is enforcing a degree of prudence in the use of union funds in election campaigns. If there is a contest between top officers in the union, their mutual surveillance also acts to restrain flagrant abuses. In the absence of an elaborate system of internal committees and line and staff organization, the president, and in some instances the secretary-treasurer, can normally exercise a broad sweep of authority over policies and finances.

The referendum was originally conceived as a check on the convention, the convention on the executive board, and the executive board—sometimes a lay executive board for this objective—on the presidency. The prevailing tendency in national union government is a negation of this design. The president, the executive board, and the convention are part of a unified system of government designed to allow the president to get things done with a minimum of interference.

Referenda may intermittently check the convention on financial matters. When the Carpenters felt excessively checked by it, they restricted the referendum.[5] Referenda in the ITU and the IAM have consistently overturned convention recommendations on financial issues. But this is a check by plebiscite which cannot be used as a technique for continuing review.

It should not be inferred that the executive board is necessarily a rubber stamp for the president's policies. On the contrary, the evidence is that not even the most autocratic president can take his board colleagues for granted. They represent sectional interests which they fully assert in executive board relationships. But the point is that the board does not conceive the essence of its responsibility to be a watchdog. Its attitude is, rather, "If the president lets me alone, I'll let him alone," and executive board members who ask too many questions are regarded as nuisances by their colleagues. Nor is the convention oriented toward guarding its general prerogatives against invasion by an overpowering executive as long as he does not make life too difficult for them by continuous dues increases. Only if there is a falling-out among the national leadership, as there has been recently in several unions, does the convention become a forum for debate over the executive power and its use. In that circumstance the executive board also becomes an agency for critical investigation of presidential performance.

The executive board is typically both a trial and appellate body in the national union's judicial process. Original jurisdiction is rather more limited, being "restricted in the main to emergency situations and offenses against the national union." [6] The common pattern of appeals procedure includes: (1) filing of charges by national authority; (2) service of charges on, and notice of trial to, the accused; (3) trial before, and decision by, the national executive board; and (4) appeal to the convention.[7]

Professor Taft has made the most probing analysis of

the national union's performance as an appellate body. His data point to the following conclusions: (1) very few cases reach it; (2) reversals and modifications of decisions of lower tribunals are frequent; (3) reversals and modifications tend to be more frequent when the penalties are heavy, involving, for example, expulsion or large fines. Professor Taft has concluded that "there is no evidence that the appellate machinery does not function effectively, that it is vain or useless. . . . The available information shows that their disciplinary machinery functions, on the whole, justly and effectively." [8]

ADMINISTRATION

By business standards most national unions do not rank high as financial enterprises. Total assets of the 250 national unions reporting to the United States Department of Labor as of September 1960 were about $785 million. Total receipts were $492 million of which $268.3 million or 54.5 percent was in dues income. Almost 10 percent of the unions had receipts of $5 million or more each. This group probably accounts for more than half the union members. Thus, the average union member, it may be said, is likely to belong to a union whose annual receipts are on the order of $5 million.[9]

In 1960, the wealthiest union was the IBEW with assets around $111 million. It was followed by the UMW with about $110 million, the ILGWU with $55 million, the IBT with $39 million, the UAW with $31 million, and the BLFME with $29 million. The IBEW also led the receipts list with approximately $65 million, followed by USW with $62 million, the UAW with $42 million, and the ITU with $23 million.[10] These figures exclude welfare and pension reserves.

A 1950 analysis of union expenditures according to purpose, by Albert Epstein, showed organizing used 32.5 percent, benefits to members 21.9 percent, administrative expense 14.5 percent, strike benefits 13.2 percent, publications (typically the monthly periodical) 6.1 percent. Accounting for less than 2 percent each are donations (1.8 percent), legal expenditures (1.5 percent), conventions (1.5 percent), research (1.3 percent), education

(0.8 percent), and political expenditures (0.2 percent). At that time, craft nationals were likely to spend a higher amount for member benefits, and industrial nationals a higher amount on organizing.[11] The administrative expense was then and is now probably incurred largely for record-keeping of membership and per capita payments.[12]

Presidential salaries and perquisites range widely. On the high side as of 1962 are: $60,000 in salary and $4,000 in expenses for the Railway Clerks president; $55,000 in salary, $17,000 allowances and $1,600 expenses for the Operating Engineers president; and $50,000 in salary and $3,400 in expenses for the UMW president. On the low side for apparently full-time officers are salaries on the order of $10,000 in the Airline Dispatchers and Brick and Clay Workers, and $7,000 to $8,000 for the presidents of the Cigar Makers, American Communications Association, Technical Engineers Association, Window Glass Cutters, and Granite Cutters.[13]

Considering the magnitude of membership and finances, the headquarters organization of the national union is not only simple, as has been said, but is also on the modest side. A typical national union has "departments" performing four classes of functions: (a) the executive and administrative function of collective bargaining and administration of personnel; (b) the internal housekeeping function of audit and finance; (c) the field function of organizing and servicing; and (d) the technical staff functions of research, education, law, publications, and public relations. A few national unions are additionally involved in auxiliary business functions.

The executive and administrative group normally consists of the president and some assistants, and an executive (or first) vice-president who functions directly under the president, the secretary-treasurer, who is in charge of the finances of the national union. In some headquarters there are vice-presidents with special responsibility for organizing and for collective bargaining in special branches of the union's jurisdiction. These responsibilities frequently may be handled below the vice-presidential level by senior staff. The most numerous group in the headquarters is the financial department with its auditors, clerks, and data processing personnel. The field staff, commonly called international representatives, is stationed in regional headquarters.

Most unions employ a small corps of technical and professional specialists in law, economic research, education, publications, and public relations. The larger unions are likely to employ, in addition, specialists in industrial engineering, international affairs, health insurance and pensions, and investments. The legal and insurance functions may be performed by outside consultants employed on a retainer basis.[14]

Most of the staff departments, except for a very few large unions—UAW, Steel, IAM, Teamsters—are one-man departments. In some unions, research and education are carried on jointly by one professional. The legal department of the national union is the only staff department which, depending on the union, is influential in deciding the substance of union policy. Lawyers have been very important, for example, in steel, rubber, brewery, and some maritime unions, and intermittently important, for example, in the garment unions and textiles. The other staff technicians usually function as technical assistants in their respective fields with relatively little influence on central policy. Once in a while, however, a research director occupies a strategic policy role.[15]

The auxiliary business functions of unions include banking, an important aspect of union activity in the 1920's, but now limited to two banks sponsored by the Amalgamated Clothing Workers union in Chicago and New York City. In recent years, middle income housing and insurance have been the significant enterprise interests of the national unions. "Five labor organizations, with government assistance, have sponsored sixty-three nonprofit projects (completed and planned) housing 51,000 families whose incomes are too high to qualify them for public housing and too low to buy good housing built for profit in the private market." [16] In the health and insurance field, national unions and subordinate bodies manage or sponsor such enterprises as group health care centers (UMW, ACWA, ILGWU, Teamsters, Hotel and Restaurant Workers) and insurance companies (the vast operations of the railroad unions, ACWA and IBEW).[17]

The elaborate staff structure of the UAW is exceptional,

reflecting the larger public stage on which this union characteristically functions. Three kinds of departments are maintained: collective bargaining, technical, and special interests.

UAW Staff Departments

COLLECTIVE BARGAINING DEPARTMENTS	TECHNICAL AND ADMINISTRATIVE DEPARTMENTS
Aerospace	Citizenship
Agricultural Implement	Community Relations
Alcoa	Community Services
American Motors	Education
Bendix	Fair Practices and
Borg-Warner	Anti-Discrimination
Briggs Beauty Ware	International Affairs
Budd	Leadership Studies
Champion Spark Plug	Legal
Chrysler	Legislative
Continental Motors	Manpower Development and
Dana	Training
Die Casting	Organizing
Doehler-Jarvis	Radio
Eaton	Recreation
Electric Storage Battery	Research
Eltra	Social Security
Ford	Special Projects
Foundry	Time Study and Engineering
General Motors	
Houdaille Industries	DEPARTMENTS FOR
Kelsey Hayes	SPECIAL INTEREST GROUPS
Mack Truck	
McQuay-Norris	Office and Professional
Spring Council	Older and Retired Workers
Studebaker	Skilled Trades
Walker	Technical
	Veterans
	Women's Auxiliaries
	Women

SOURCE: Walter P. Reuther, *Report of the President,* Part 3, 19th UAW Constitutional Convention, March 20–27, 1964, pp. 3–4.

NATIONALS AND LOCALS

Constitutionally, as has been seen, the local and inter-mediate bodies are subordinate to the national union. Operationally, the degree of subordination varies within the union by function and by unions. The functional relationships enforced by the national union on the subordinate bodies can be grouped under five headings: (1) a control relationship in which the national union replaces or displaces the subordinate body in the exercise of a function; (2) a review relationship in which the subordinate body performs the function subject to periodic scrutiny, inspection, or audit and instruction; (3) an appellate relationship in which the national union acts as a formal line of appeal from decisions of subordinate bodies; (4) a service relationship in which the national union provides guidance, counsel, and analysis on request; and (5) a "laissez-faire" relationship, in which there are almost no functional links between the national and subordinate bodies except for the transmission of per capita payments and receipts.

A national market tends to induce national union direction or control over the negotiation of the basic terms of the collective bargaining agreement. Important examples are the corporation-wide agreements in automobiles, aircraft, basic steel, rubber, and electrical appliances. In the pattern or standard agreement, the national union negotiates a model contract which in its main features is intended to set the standard for all relevant agreements negotiated by subordinate bodies. Deviations from the pattern, however, are common.[18] Jurisdiction policy in the craft-based unions is increasingly subject to control by the national union, as in the Carpenters where "power over jurisdiction has been completely centralized," but enforcement here is likely to be uneven.[19] The national union also controls the jurisdiction of the subordinate bodies, especially the locals as against each other.

National control over the internal government of subordinate bodies is most plainly evidenced in trusteeship. Trusteeship—sometimes also known as "supervision" or "receivership"—is a procedure whereby the national union sets aside the self-government of a subordinate body in favor of a trustee wholly or partly under national direction. The trustee is most often an officer of the national union, but it is not uncommon for him to be a local union officer acting in behalf of the national. The function of trusteeship is to give the national union a direct weapon to enforce compliance against a recalcitrant subordinate body. The circumstances which commonly give rise to the legitimate use of trusteeship are when the subordinate body willfully fails to conform to established standards of honesty, efficient and effective management of finances, orderly constitutional government, adherence to contracts, and protection of local union assets from schismatic or secessionist movements.[20]

Most trusteeship provisions do not explicitly protect the rights and interests of subordinate bodies during the trusteeship or specify the conditions under which local government is to be restored. The national executive's decision to install a trustee is usually subject to appeal to the convention.

LMRDA requires that trusteeship must be in accord with the union constitution, and that the purposes must be restricted to dealing with corruption, compliance with the collective agreement, restoration of democracy, "or otherwise legitimate objects." Procedures are established for reporting the trusteeship, conserving the assets, and voting the delegates from the trusteed local (Title III). The regulation of trusteeships under LMRDA was the product of evidence that the mechanism was being used by national union administration as an instrument of reprisal against opposition elements, to control the votes of the subordinate body in the convention in favor of the incumbent national leadership, and to mulct the local treasury.

The most frequently reported reasons for trusteeship were: (1) the establishment of a caretaker government to deal with the situation where "the subordinate body cannot function autonomously, usually because of conditions beyond its control; (2) dissension, i.e., where the national union takes over "because of disruptive factionalism, other than that caused by advocates for disaffiliation"; and (3) secession, where trusteeship was imposed "because of actual or threatened secession" by the subordinate body from the national.[21] After two and one-half years of experience with the trusteeship provisions of the law, the Secretary of Labor concluded:

1. Establishment of trusteeships has never been a widespread practice, except in a few unions. When the Act became effective, trusteeships existed in less than 1 percent of the covered unions. Now, less than half that percentage were involved.

2. The Act was effective in correcting the malpractices disclosed by the McClellan Committee. Further, a large number of trusteeships, while not corrupt, were unnecessarily continued and have now been terminated.

3. Since enactment of the law, many national union constitutions have been amended to provide greater safeguards against unnecessary suspension of autonomy.

4. Indications are that the act had not substantially hindered unions from establishing essential trusteeships.

5. The reporting and disclosure of the facts surrounding trusteeships, and the active cooperation of the vast majority of unions and union officers, resulted in substantial compliance with the law with a minimum need for enforcement.[22]

The major processes of subordinate bodies which are constitutionally subject to systematic review by the national union are the collective agreement, the strike, and internal financial administration.[23] If there is no immediate larger interest involved in local collective bargaining, the review by the national union tends to be mechanical, and disapproval of contracts is very unusual.[24]

Strike review is taken seriously because strike benefits are likely to be paid from funds under national union control, and the strike itself may subject the national to financial liability.[25] The national union's audit of local books looks for possible misappropriation of funds and remission of per capita on the full local membership.[26] The appellate function of the national discussed earlier exemplifies another sort of review function.

The servicing function of the national union consists of assisting in collective bargaining negotiations, augmenting local representation in the later stages of the grievance procedure and arbitration, and mediating internal union conflicts and conflicts between the local union leadership and management. The servicing function in collective bargaining is especially useful in connection with technical issues in health insurance, pensions, industrial engineering standards, and technological change problems.

The factory locals are more likely to use the national's service than are the non-factory crafts. The exception is the railroad unions where the integrated nature of the railroad economy and the importance of the insurance function make for a continuously interacting service relationship. Local unions tend to criticize the national's servicing because there is not enough of it. "What are we paying per capita to the International for?" is the way the criticism is usually expressed.

History, economics, attitudes, tactics, and needs combine to shape the nature of the national-local relationship. Historically, what matters is whether the union organization evolved out of local efforts or from a nationally directed organizing campaign. One may expect in the former a continuing habit of self-reliance, and in the latter a habit of dependence on the "international representative."

Power enhancement by a strong leader on either side will affect the national-local relationship. Hoffa is an example of a union president who is seeking to enlarge the influence of the national union over the subordinate bodies. Conversely, strong local leaders in the Teamsters are not without effective defenses in resisting the expansion of national union authority over their affairs.[27] It is not uncommon in many unions for a secure local leadership to effectively bar from its territory national union representatives who are *persona non grata*.[28]

A local union bargaining in a national product market will necessarily rely more heavily on the national union than will a local union bargaining in a local or regional market. An industry or a plant undergoing rapid technological change sets forces in motion which local unions are incapable of dealing with on their own power.

The employer is not without interest or power in influencing the national-local relationship. Part of the price which an employer has been known to exact in return for a livable relationship with the local union is the exclusion of the national to avoid the injection of "international policy" into the bargaining.[29] More commonly, the management under economic stress may find the national union more "responsible" and hence encourage national intervention.

LEADERSHIP

National union leaders, especially the presidents, as has been seen, have great constitutional and *de facto* power. But, with a few notable exceptions, this great power is exercised within narrow limits set by continuously impinging political, economic, and public policy constraints. In consequence, the quality of national union leadership is more often than not a secondary rather than a primary influence on the union's fortunes. It is probably at the height of its effects in the initial rather than the later period of the union-management relationship.[30]

National unions in the United States are characteristically broadly based alliances of different group interests. As Gosta Rehn, the Swedish trade union economist, has perceptively observed, "The enlargement of unions makes them weaker against internal pressures for equity." [31] The greater the range of interests, the greater "the internal pressure for equity" and the narrower, therefore, the zone of maneuverability. Rival union interests impose an additional constraint on union leaders. Economic constraints arise from the fact that even the most powerful and brilliant union leadership have, in the long run, no recourse against reduced demand for manpower induced by technological change, shifts in consumer tastes, or cyclical fluctuations in the economy. The constraints set by public policy are many. Wage-price policies and strike restrictions, for example, diminish the zone of union discretion in collective bargaining and in internal union administration.

A few national union leaders have been able to transcend the inherent limitations of their office and function by the force of their individual abilities and personalities. In recent decades, Walter Reuther, John L. Lewis, James

R. Hoffa, Harry Bridges, Sidney Hillman, James Petrillo, Joseph Beirne, and James Carey, for example, have, in different ways and varying durations, managed to imprint their individual styles on their national unions and the conduct of industrial relations.

More than any other modern national labor leader, Reuther has attempted to bring rational planning and a social philosophy to the practice of unionism. The automobile industry, profitable and dynamic, has provided a favorable setting for the exercise of talents which have enabled him to bring about what may be styled a welfare standard rather than a commodity standard in the employment of workers.[32] Nor is the luster of Reuther's performance dimmed by the fact that automobile managements have seized the bargaining initiative rather frequently in recent years, for even when this happened, their debt to Reuther's tutelage was unmistakable. On the union administration side, Reuther's distinctive contribution has been to enlarge the vision of his membership by effective leadership at the same time that he has tried to be responsive to their shop and job concerns.

John L. Lewis is probably the only other national union leader in the very top-drawer class, but for a much shorter time, in a more limited area, and in a much less favorable economic environment. Lewis' creative accomplishment, achieved under adverse economic circumstances, was his indispensable role in organizing the mass production industries from his base in the UMW during the middle 1930's. This set in motion a profound transformation of employment administration in modern American industry. The evidence on Lewis' performance in coal industry bargaining is mixed. In internal union administration, no national union has experienced a tighter personal control than Lewis was able to impose on the UMW.

The measure of Hoffa as a national union leader is the proficiency with which he perfected a governmental control structure to centralize an essentially decentralized union, and the tough singlemindedness with which he used his personal power to assimilate the subordinate bodies and leaders into this control structure. This achievement had its price in detaching the Teamsters from the family of unions and bringing it under continuing government surveillance.[33]

Harry Bridges of the West Coast Longshoremen abandoned a heritage of violence, conflict, radicalism, and class struggle to institute a joint regime of union-employer collaboration. This regime has sought to ameliorate the adverse effects of technology upon the longshoremen and to release employers from restrictions imposed by outdated work rules. The paradox is that Bridges' involvement in one of the most ambitious—and possibly one of the most effective—experiments in "class collaboration" has not appreciably affected his radical ideology.[34]

Joseph Beirne's distinction derives from his massive effort to transform the organization of telephone workers from a highly fragmented company unionism into a coherent national union structure which gives the workers the sort of power base needed to confront their great corporate antagonist. The quality of his achievement is enhanced by the CWA's essential democracy which forced Beirne and his associates to argue through and justify every increment in power grudgingly yielded to the national union by local and regional unions.[35] As yet, however, Beirne has not made a comparably significant breakthrough in collective bargaining with the Bell system.

James Suffridge of the Retail Clerks has transformed a sleepy, ineffectual, decentralized, and, in some local areas, racket-ridden union into a modern union. Modernization has consisted of the "growth of functions and power in the International Office . . . and the international itself has its center in the office of the presidency." [36] This process of union centralization has been a response to the centralizing forces in retailing. The expansion of the national role has included growth in organizing staff and, to a lesser degree, in technical staff. Although the union is far from having organized anything like the majority of workers in its jurisdiction, it has made important strides toward this goal. Suffridge's dynamic view of the union's needs has been a decisive factor in its growth.

James Carey's primary accomplishment was his relentless struggle to win an industry's employees from an effective but communist-oriented national trade union leadership. All other cases in which communist control of a union deteriorated came about from a falling-out among the insiders. Carey is the only national union leader who was able to bring such a development about from the outside of a ruling communist group.

The late Sidney Hillman's insights into the integrative, positive role of a union in a competitive, seasonal, and unstable industry added an important dimension to trade unionism in the United States. Hillman's Amalgamated Clothing Workers was not alone or even first in establishing a rule of equity based on union power. The International Ladies' Garment Workers under Morris Sigman, Benjamin Schlesinger, and David Dubinsky had also evolved to the point at which Hillman arrived. All of them perceived that union defensiveness alone was not adequate in the sort of industry which, if left to the behavior of individual employers, would be destroyed as a viable enterprise capable of providing a decent livelihood for its workers. Only the unions in the needle trades, it was clear—not the employers—had the capabilities and the perspective to maintain these industries as going concerns. Hillman's distinction is that he not only practiced this form of "labor statesmanship"—to use a phrase which had meaning when applied to Hillman but which has subsequently been corrupted—but he also articulated it in a striking, reflective, and literate style.[37] The quality of the needle trades unions' achievements can be appreciated by contrast with the seasonal, casual, small-scale East Coast longshore industry, which has not been able to surmount racketeering and chaos.

POLITICS

Recently, political turmoil has erupted in national unions, most of which had been regarded as safe for incumbent presidents. Within a two-year period, David J. McDonald of the Steelworkers, James Carey of the IUE, and Arnold Zander of the AFSCME have been defeated for reelection. Charles Cogen, although he was not opposed by an incumbent AFT president, ran against and defeated an incumbent president's choice. Hotly contested campaigns have taken place in the Textile Workers, the American Federation of Government Employees, Insurance Workers, Machinists, and Longshoremen (ILA).[38]

In most of these contests the personal style of the president, at least at first, became the main focus of opposition rather than any serious difference over policy. McDonald was never able to achieve the common touch of Philip Murray, his revered predecessor, and his style of life, more than any large defect in his policies, was undoubtedly the chief element in his defeat by I. W. Abel, the secretary-treasurer, who has come closer to being a man of the masses. Substantive issues, however, were not completely ignored in the election campaign. McDonald stressed his "bread and butter" accomplishments for the members; Abel stressed the return of collective bargaining to the members from the remoteness of McDonald's exclusive meetings with technicians and top managements. But McDonald's fall was ultimately caused by what has been called "tuxedo unionism."

Carey's defeat must also be attributed in large part to personal qualities. His ungovernable temper, contentiousness, and "vindictiveness"—which probably also contributed to the disturbed state of industrial relations in the industry—were increasingly directed toward his union colleagues, most of them old comrades in the anti-communist wars. More in affection than in reproval, Murray Kempton remarked of Carey, "it is his nature to affront everyone." [39] There was a tragic element in Carey's defeat. Carey was one of the early founders of the CIO. He had carried on an unremitting struggle against the UE leadership from his base as CIO secretary-treasurer. When the communist-dominated unions were expelled and UE departed from the CIO, Carey led the newly-established IUE in a bruising and ultimately victorious attack on UE's dominance in the electrical products industry. Few observers of the union scene could bring themselves to believe that Carey could have known that the vote which at first seemed to reelect him as president of the IUE in 1965 had been manipulated, and that his rival, Paul Jennings, had in fact won the election.

The thrust of opposition in the AFSCME was directed more against Arnold Zander's chief assistant than against Zander himself. Zander was portrayed as a man who was being manipulated by a Machiavelli. Almost all of the opposition came from men whom Zander brought into the union and who, at least in their early careers, had risen to importance under his tutelage and direction.

One may speculate that McDonald and Carey could have continued in office indefinitely, "warts and all," if the tide of collective bargaining events had run smoothly. But the collective bargaining climate was being altered by economic developments after 1957 which, on balance, weakened union and strengthened management power—particularly in the mass production and transportation industries. This suggests that the personal qualities or inadequacies of leaders—real or imagined—which may have been tolerable earlier could not be accepted when the union experienced stress. Yet, the sources of the eruptions in the public employee union are in part to be found in the change from an adverse to a favorable climate.[40]

In steel, changes in technology, management strategy, and employment combined after 1957 to strengthen the management side in negotiations. The union membership was dominated by a profound pessimism about employment prospects. This unfavorable drift of events, including a substantial decline in union membership, gave criticisms of McDonald as a person a sharper cutting edge than in the past, when McDonald's designee for executive vice-president was opposed by a member of the inner circle; and in 1957 McDonald himself faced a rank-and-file rival who captured more than a third of the vote.[41]

The IUE's record in membership growth has been viewed as being substantially below the potential in the dynamically growing industries comprising the IUE jurisdiction. Unlike other mass production unions which had come upon leaner days, it was only after 1957 that the IUE was unable to take the measure of its chief antagonist, General Electric. In AFSCME, as has been noted, it was because the prospects for public employee collective bargaining began to improve that Zander's defects as a union leader loomed larger. A similar development appears to have played a significant role in the AFT election which brought Charles Cogen into the presidency of the union.

The recent contests for national office were without exception between top leaders. McDonald was defeated by the national secretary-treasurer; Carey by a sub-district director; Zander by a national board member and district council head; and the choice of the incumbent president was defeated by the president of the largest and most militant local in the AFT—the New York Teachers.

A contested referendum election of national officers of the kind witnessed in USW and IUE split the leadership group wide open, and converted it for the duration into massive campaign committees. Before LMRDA, the incumbent national leadership overtly utilized all of the union's resources in their behalf. The journal of the national union frequently ignored the rival and became a campaign vehicle for boosting the incumbent's election stock. No staff member was permitted neutrality in these contests. Dismissal was the likely price of neutrality or of aiding the unsuccessful candidate—a situation which has not been changed materially by LMRDA.

LMRDA's most significant achievement may turn out to be the obstacles it has put in the way of appropriating the union's manpower and money for partisan campaign purposes. Even so, the law is not able to completely control the improper use of union assets. Reaching one million members by mail costs $50,000 for postage alone. The money has to be found somewhere, and levies on union staff members have become an increasing source of campaign funds to partially offset the loss of union resources since LMRDA.

The national union has not been able to develop rules so that elections are conducted equitably. The areas which appear to require attention are the use of union staff for internal partisanship on union time, the use of the union journal as the organ of the administration or president in power, and the irresponsibility of campaign propaganda.

CHAPTER VIII

The AFL-CIO—
The Government of a Federation

This is an examination of the American Federation of Labor
and Congress of Industrial Organizations (AFL-CIO) as the
government of a federation.[1] The AFL-CIO occupies the
high point in the pyramid of union government in the
United States, but its power is no greater in the last
analysis than the national unions are willing to grant it.
The AFL-CIO as an association of unions is thus truly a
federation.

The history of experimentation with forms of union
association begins with the founding of the National Trades
Union in 1834. From the National Trades Union to the
Knights of Labor the important constituencies of these
associations were local central bodies. The formation of
the American Federation of Labor in 1886 was unique because it marked a shift to autonomous national unions as
the primary constituents of the national association of
unions. The AFL persevered where the earlier associations
had not, precisely because it had tied itself to the as-
cendant national union power in the American scheme of
union government.[2]

It seemed at first that the CIO, under forceful leaders like John L. Lewis and, later, Philip Murray, would depart from type and subordinate the national to the federation. This tendency lasted only so long as the national unions had to depend on the CIO and on the Miners for personnel and financing. When the national unions began to stand on their own, the tutelage of the CIO diminished. Philip Murray continued to exert influence on the national unions, but this was personal rather than organizational, and in any case not constitutional. Walter Reuther's accession at Murray's death late in 1952 marked the end of the period of CIO protectorship.

COMPOSITION OF THE FEDERATION

The federation is, most importantly, an association of 130 unions.[3] In addition, the AFL-CIO is composed of city central bodies (773), state federations (50 and Puerto Rico), trade and industrial departments (7) and directly affiliated local unions (299 with 62,000 members).[4] The national federation, directed by an elected president and secretary-treasurer, is administratively organized into fifteen headquarters departments and twenty-three regional offices.

The central bodies and the trade departments constitute two types of subfederation. Central bodies in the cities and states are composed of the locals of federation-affiliated national unions in the respective states and localities. The "trade" departments of the AFL-CIO—Railway Employees, Metal Trades, Building and Construction Trades, Maritime Trades, Industrial Union, Union Label and Service Trades, and, most recently, Food and Beverage —bring together national unions affiliated with the federation by a common interest in the trades or industries suggested by the name of the department. The departments in turn charter subordinate local councils. (In the Railway Employees' Department the local councils are called "system federations.") The local councils of the departments are made up of locals of the national unions affiliated with the national department.

The directly affiliated local unions—known as federal labor unions in the AFL, and local industrial unions in the

CIO—are locals which are not attached to a national union; hence the federation functions in place of a national union. This is regarded as a transitional stage until the directly affiliated local union is brought into an established or newly formed national. Some national unions began by bringing together directly affiliated locals. The directly affiliated local union may be affiliated with a "council," which is a loose confederation of locals—not quite a department —in a given industry grouping. In 1963, the councils were the Agricultural Workers Organizing Committee and the Matchworkers Council.

The trade and industrial departments have pursued three broad objectives: (1) protection of the department's corporate jurisdictional interests through pressure-group activities in government and within the federation; (2) coordination of activities of affiliated unions in organizing, collective bargaining, legislation, and information; and (3) for two departments—building trades and industrial union—adjudication of rivalry among affiliates.[5]

The central body is primarily concerned with political and legislative functions in its territory, and provides limited aid to local affiliates in collective bargaining. A well-established city central may also be influential in resolving jurisdictional difficulties.

In a very real sense, then, the federation is not a conventional union in its own right, because it does not engage in collective bargaining or have individual members—except for the directly affiliated locals, with respect to which the federation partakes of the functions of a national union. The federation is primarily an association of unions, and more particularly an association of national unions.

FORMAL GOVERNMENT

The supreme organ of the federation is the biennial convention, composed primarily but not exclusively of delegates from the affiliated national unions with voting weight determined by the national unions' per capita payments to the federation. The per capita payment is 7 cents a month, supplemented from time to time by temporary assessments which constitute about 80 percent of the federation's income. The next largest source of income—on the order of 10 percent— is per capita and other payments made by the directly affiliated local unions.[6]

The convention provides a national spotlight for the federation and a meeting ground for the labor movement's top leadership, while serving as a plebiscitary body and a debaters' forum. Alignments on controversial issues are pretty well determined off the convention floor, but the convention registers the votes and the supporting debate. Occasionally, it provides the pressure of urgency required to resolve a particular issue. Thus, in 1961, the convention, with its pressures, established a situation in which President Meany inched through an internal disputes program between the building trades and the industrial unions, and provided the staging ground for an easing of strained relations on the civil rights issue.

Effective authority in the AFL-CIO is exercised by an executive council composed of twenty-seven vice-presidents and the president and secretary-treasurer. An executive committee of the executive council functions as an agenda or steering committee. The president, secretary-treasurer, and executive council are elected by the convention at large. On political, but not constitutional grounds, council members are likely to be chosen to represent: (1) the very largest unions; (2) strategic industry groupings, such as the building trades or public employees; (3) the balance between former AFL and former CIO unions; and (4), most recently, Negro trade union interests.

A constitutionally established General Board consists of the principal officer of each national union affiliate. The only clue which the constitution provides to the functions of this board is that it "shall decide all policy questions referred to it by the Executive Officers or by the Executive Council." [7] Apart from this, the constitution is silent on the position of the General Board in relation to the Executive Council. In practice, the General Board is a forum for giving expression to and gaining wider acceptance of important policies of the federation. Thus, the Board is a major policy-approving body rather than a policy-formulating body.

The constitution provides for specified committees

and staff departments.* Appointment to the staff of the departments and the membership of the committees is the prerogative of the president. In practice, the staff is appointed by department heads in consultation with the president. The committee is, in general, a policy advisory group, and the staff department is a headquarters administrative unit. The exception is the Committee on Political Education (COPE), which is primarily an operating unit with both a headquarters and a field staff. The Organizing Department has a permanent field staff of 154, assigned to twenty-three regions, each under a regional director.

The locus of effective power in the federation at present is the executive council, which is a barometer of major internal federation pressures and counter-pressures. As president of the AFL-CIO, George Meany carries great weight in the council, but on issues involving union interests, as distinguished from public policy interests, he has to fight to maintain a position of influence. Council debate is often intense and occasionally bitter. The men who make up the council are accustomed to power in their own organizations, and are not disposed to act as rubber stamps, even with as determined a person as Meany.

REPRESENTATION—POLITICS AND LEGISLATION

The federation meets a need for cohesiveness, collaboration, and solidarity on the part of its constituent

---

* The committees are designated as Legislation, Civil Rights, Political Education, Ethical Practices, International Affairs, Education, Social Security, Economic Policy, Community Services, Housing, Research, Public Relations, Safety and Occupational Health, Veterans' Affairs, Investment, and Organization.

The headquarters staff departments are Auditing, Civil Rights, Community Services Activities, Education, International Affairs, Investment, Legislation, Organization, Political Education, Public Relations, Publications, Research, Social Insurance, General Counsel, and Library.

In addition to these formal departments, individual staff members are assigned to coordinate state and local central bodies and to assist the president and secretary-treasurer in a variety of special responsibilities.[8]

elements. Even in the absence of a prevailing socialist ideology, solidarity is an article of working-class faith, and it is nurtured by a national labor center. For example, the president of an important national union observed, "We derive our moral and spiritual sustenance from being an integral part of the entire labor movement." [9] This need for solidarity is re-enforced by a feeling which most union leaders have of still being outside of the main status groups of the society. Affiliation with the federation confers public legitimacy. Thus, while Teamster President Hoffa can boast of his union's successes as an independent, he and his colleagues still maintain a campaign for readmission into the federation. True, there are unions which hold that they are free from the ideological and economic encumbrances which burden the labor movement as a whole, but they are rare exceptions. [10]

The AFL-CIO undertakes to exercise seven classes of function: (1) administrating personnel and finances; (2) representing the labor movement's interests in public policy and the international labor movements; (3) "organizing the unorganized"; (4) policing the observance of "ethical practices" and civil rights standards by affiliates; (5) resolving jurisdictional conflict among affiliates; (6) servicing affiliates in their research, education, and industrial engineering needs; and (7) communicating federation policy to the union membership and the public at large.

The representative function is two-fold. In the first instance, it expresses the federation's role as the symbol of and spokesman for all member unions on questions of public policy. [11] This role is supported by a large headquarters technical staff in Washington, consisting of specialists in every major public policy area. Their range of specialization is suggested by the titles of the staff departments (see p. 104*n*.).

In few fields has the outlook of the federation changed so fundamentally as it has toward legislative and political action, which continues to be the most important form of representation. To be sure, federations have always been active in legislation and politics, but until 1933 the main emphasis was defense against specific obstacles and injustices, such as the labor injunction and the "yellow dog" contract. Even after 1933, the serious political efforts of the labor movement, except for a few national unions, were aimed at such pressure-group objectives as repeal of the Taft-Hartley Law and "right to work" laws. The CIO, to be sure, brought program and spirit to legislation and politics, but they lacked systematic organizational expression.

The profound alteration in the labor-movement program is found in the central place now assigned to broad questions of public policy. If the union spokesmen were to borrow words from economists, they might say that their collective bargaining efforts today can have only "micro" effects, while the vexing problems of a complex economy can be dealt with only through "macro" techniques and measures. As the unions see it, only the federal government is capable of dealing with these problems.

This broadening of labor's public policy interest from pressure group to program is suggested by an observation of Andrew J. Biemiller, director of legislative activities of the AFL-CIO, when speaking about the 1960 campaign:

> As a practical matter there was no "labor issue"—you will note that I am using the singular—in this campaign. There was no attempt on the part of the labor movement to make a rallying-point or a *cause célèbre* out of the Landrum-Griffin act; nor was there any disposition on the part of our opponents to make the labor movement a special target . . . President Meany and most of the labor people felt that in terms of the national interest, many other matters were of far greater importance—and in all candor, likely to be far more effective campaign issues.[12]

In the 1965 congressional session the federation launched a substantial campaign for both "medicare" and the repeal of Taft-Hartley section 14B, which would have the effect of repealing the state right-to-work laws. It would be difficult to estimate on which—one a public policy issue and the other a pressure-group issue—the federation worked harder. It is no accident that George Meany as federation president is one of the most influential men in the councils of a national Democratic administration. The labor movement is a major (if not *the* major) force for the broad range of welfare and social legislation in the federal and state legislatures.

The political and legislative interests of the AFL-CIO are organized into a network consisting of the national federation's COPE and Legislative Department; a headquarters corps of technical specialists in economics, civil rights, labor law, atomic energy, education, and international affairs in the AFL-CIO headquarters; full-time lobbyists and political departments in the AFL-CIO affiliates; and the state and local arms of the federation. The organizational network engages in propaganda, education and training of labor's political workers, lobbying, registration campaigns, polling surveys, and the strategic application of union manpower and money in behalf of individual candidates. The labor movement's political activists show up in caucuses at political conventions, as insiders within the major parties, and as candidates and office holders.

The federation's main activities in legislative programs other than labor legislation have been to support and reenforce, not to initiate. Once a program is conceived—and this is more true nationally and during Democratic administrations—the labor movement's technicians will be active participants in drafting, massing legislative support, and, if the program is enacted, in maintaining a permanent vigil over its administration. If not enacted, then the labor movement will be the chief prod for further efforts. Minimum wages, Medicare, social security, and civil rights are the contemporary cases in point.

Another representative function of the federation is its effort to assert and stake out a recognized place for the labor movement in the power structure of the national and the local communities. This is symbolized, even if not always realized, in the matter-of-course involvement of a federation spokesman in almost every labor-related committee and social agency established at any level of government and community organization. A Community Services Department organizes and directs this labor interest in social welfare.[13]

REPRESENTATION—INTERNATIONAL

The second aspect of the federation's representative functions is international. Measured by the proportion of income spent, the federation's activity in the international labor movement and in international affairs is one of its most important functions.[14] The importance of the federation's international role can be gauged also by the serious engagement in it of the president and other influential members of the executive council, and by the intensity of disagreement which it induces. A Department of International Affairs is manned by a staff of specialists working in Washington and around the world. Staff members are assigned to represent federation interests at the International Confederation of Free Trade Unions (ICFTU) in Brussels, the Organization for Economic Cooperation and Development (OECD) in Paris, and the International Labor Organization (ILO) in Geneva. An auxiliary effort is the American Institute for Free Labor Development additionally financed by private business contributions and United States government contracts. The main purpose is the training of Latin-American trade union leaders in the United States and in several educational centers throughout Latin America.[15] A comparable effort is the African-American Labor Center, which concentrates "on projects in vocational training, workers' education, cooperatives, health clinics, and housing." [16]

The federation's international role has the following five interdependent objectives in which the dominant theme is the preservation of a strong anti-communist position: (1) the maintenance of a position of American power in the ICFTU, related international bodies, and the world labor movement; (2) a running assessment of United States foreign policy positions, and active consultation to this end with the State Department and other agencies in international work; (3) direct assistance to foreign labor movements under siege by or in opposition to communist forces; (4) the training of foreign trade unionists in the organizational skills and in protection against communist penetration—notably in Latin America and to some degree in Africa; (5) the recommendation, and not infrequently the right of approval, of government personnel to deal with international labor matters.

The relationship of the AFL-CIO to the international labor movement generates more controversy than any other issue except jurisdiction. The sources of controversy are found in policies, administration, and personalities.

Meany has set the ICFTU fight against communism as the keystone of federation policy in the international labor movement in stating that it "deserves our paramount attention because it involves the very existence of free trade unionism." [17] Meany has been critical of ICFTU leadership because in his view it has not been sufficiently vigorous and resourceful in its anti-communist offensive. He has also been outspoken in his criticism of the quality and effectiveness of ICFTU administration. This mistrust of ICFTU has undoubtedly influenced the federation to establish trade union aid programs bilaterally with other national labor centers; this Meany has defended on the ground that these activities "complement rather than supplant the work of the world organization."

Walter Reuther and his brother, Victor, the head of the UAW international program, are probably the leading critics of Meany on this issue within the federation. Their views do not, of course, stem from any affinity for communist interests. The Reuthers have been protagonists in the anti-communist wars in the UAW and in the CIO for more than thirty years. Their criticisms are directed mainly against what they hold to be the intemperateness and impulsiveness of Meany's adverse assessment of the ICFTU, and against the influence exercised by Jay Lovestone upon Meany in the formulation of international policy. Leader of the American Communist Party a generation ago, but since that time a committed and active anti-communist, Lovestone is viewed by his opponents as "a sinister figure" exerting "a rigid and essentially negative" influence.[18] His supporters, however, regard him as "a brilliant man, vastly knowledgeable about communist affairs throughout the world . . . [with] an extraordinary network of informants, with whom he keeps in close touch, and a remarkable sensitivity for developments in the communist world before they become apparent to others." [19] Both his supporters and critics agree that Lovestone plays a leading role in determining international policy and orientation of the federation.[20] The operations of the federation in Latin America under Serafino Romualdi, the most important antagonist of Latin American communism, have not inspired similar criticism within the federation.

ORGANIZING AND REGULATION

The early AFL carried on organizing activities, but with nothing like the flair and resourcefulness of the CIO in the 1935–1940 period which stands out as the golden age of union militancy.[21] Only the federation's vigorous agricultural workers' organizing campaign of the late 1950's and early 1960's resembled in concept these old CIO campaigns. Federation organizers in the present period have been used to aid organizing efforts of specific affiliates, and to assist affiliates in challenging or resisting challenges of unions expelled from the federation. At first, organizing efforts sponsored by the federation would proceed only if conflicting jurisdictional claims of national unions were adjusted—and they hardly ever were. In attempts to accelerate federation organizing, the AFL-CIO has disallowed "paper" jurisdictional claims, and has been experimenting with coordinated drives on a multi-union basis in specific areas.[22]

The federation performs a limited technical service function for the central bodies, the directly affiliated unions, and, to a lesser degree, for national unions in the fields of research and the preparation of educational materials. An investment department has been recently established to encourage and advise the national unions on their investment of pension, welfare, and trade union funds in the housing field. Recently this department has been instrumental in creating the AFL-CIO Mortgage Investment Trust "to provide a medium for a mortgage investment program." [23]

The federation's power to regulate the national unions is described in constitutional provisions requiring that affiliated unions shall be free from communism, corruption, and discrimination. To enforce these prohibitions the federation has developed an Ethical Practices Committee and a Civil Rights Committee. The Ethical Practices Committee has formulated specific codes on the issuance of local union charters, health and welfare fund administration, racketeering, "conflict of interest" business investments, financial practices, and democratic processes. Under direction of the executive council, the committee investigated charges of corruption in national union affiliates and directly affiliated locals. Their findings were subsequently upheld by the council and the convention. Remedial or disciplinary action enforced on offending affiliates has included expulsion, the chartering of and providing aid to rival unions, placing unions on probation, and installing monitors in unions.

The militant phase of the ethical practices program of the federation has run its course, largely due to three reasons: the enactment of the LMRDA; the ability of the Teamsters to survive expulsion (although others like the Laundry Workers and Bakery Workers were badly hurt by it); and the threat of secession by some of the building trades unions in the event of federation action against President Maurice Hutcheson of the Carpenters on the occasion of his difficulties with the law.[24]

The ethical practices interest of the federation constitutes the sharpest break with the historic conception of national union autonomy within the federation. But even so, the ethical practices provisions constitute a codification of the AFL's action in expelling the Longshoremen in 1953, and a constitutional expression that the autonomy principle will not be a bar to proceeding against corrupt practices by affiliates.

Communist penetration into national unions has not been a serious problem recently, although in at least one case the federation executive council held up approval of a merger pending examination of the possibility of communist control in one of the union parties to the merger. In another case the issue of communist penetration into an affiliate was considered, but no action taken. The precedent for an anti-communist provision is found in the CIO's expulsion of eleven communist-dominated unions in 1949 and 1950.[25]

The constitution contains a provision "encourag[ing] all workers without regard to race, creed, color, national origin or ancestry to share equally in the full benefits of union organizations," [26] and a section establishing enforcement through a Committee on Civil Rights. Suspension by the executive council is explicitly mentioned as a way of enforcing the ethical practices and anti-communist/anti-fascist provisions. However, there is no explicit reference in the constitution to sanctions against violators of the civil rights provision. Meany has distinguished between corruption and discrimination as grounds for expulsion of affiliates:

> . . . Corruption—like communism—seizes the leadership of a union and works down to lower levels by perverting the union's democratic procedures. The rank-and-file members are not consciously affected in their daily lives. They don't know what's going on, and they tend to dismiss published charges against the leadership as just another attack by a normally hostile press. Expulsion was the only way to convince the membership of this domination by corrupt elements. In most cases the members then rallied to new, clean unions or have overthrown the old leadership.

> But there is a big difference between corruption and discrimination. Discrimination is resisted at the top but perpetrated below. Discrimination represents the wrong-headedness of rank-and-file members; it is often maintained by unimpeachably democratic processes.

> Would we be better off to cast out these misguided members and remove them from the influence of the mainstream of the labor movement, meanwhile expelling in the same action the national leaders who deplore and fight discrimination? I think not. I think we can do more toward educating them if they're in the federation, with their own leaders getting broad AFL-CIO support toward the same end.[27]

The federation has manifested increased sensitivity to civil rights issues in recent years. At the federation's 1959 convention, Meany demanded to know from A. Philip Randolph "who in hell nominated you the guardian of all the Negroes in America?" In 1961, the executive council "censured" Randolph. At the 1963 convention, civil rights was the main item on the agenda, and Meany referred to Randolph, who led off the discussion, as "our own Phil Randolph."[28]

The federation's Civil Rights Department has been strengthened. The department has encouraged affiliates "to develop and operate an affirmative equal-job-opportunity program within the trade or industry covered by the union and to deal in a positive way with the problems of discrimi-

nation within the union itself," and to assign "at least
one skilled staff member for service on call in community-
wide programs to end discrimination." [29] In addition, the
department conducts civil rights training programs and
issues educational materials. Professor Ray Marshall, an
authority on the subject, concludes that "particularly important progress seems to have been made in the elimination of segregated locals." [30] Meany's judgment that AFL-
CIO "influence was decisive in expanding the original civil
rights bill . . . to include a fair employment practices
section" [31] appears to be supported by evidence.[32] However, Herbert Hill, the labor secretary of the NAACP, does
not agree that progress has been made—he maintains that
"the AFL-CIO is becoming more conservative and increasingly basing itself upon the narrow and restrictive craft
unions." [33]

REGULATION OF JURISDICTIONAL DISPUTES

The merger between the AFL and the CIO could not
have taken place if it had had to wait on the settlement of
rival jurisdictional claims between AFL and CIO affiliates.
Unity was entered into with constitutional recognition that
concurrent and overlapping jurisdictions did in fact exist.[34]
Before formal unity was consummated a trial concord was
set up in the form of a no-raiding agreement which pledged
each signatory to respect "the established bargaining relationship" of every other signatory of the other federation.
Later, the concept of "established bargaining relationship"
was incorporated in the AFL-CIO constitution. The word
"jurisdiction" is used in the constitution, but it is given no
operative meaning.

The search for a viable formula to achieve jurisdictional amity among affiliates has a long history in the
AFL, and has been a continuing source of controversy and
irritation within the AFL-CIO from its very inception. Fratri-
cidal warfare may cut more deeply than warfare against
strangers, and in some respects feeling over jurisdiction
worsened after unity.

The 1961 convention adopted a new constitutional
Article, XXI, incorporating procedures for the settlement
of internal disputes. This Article states the standards of

equity for judging jurisdictional contests—namely, "the established collective bargaining relationship" and "the established work relationship." The established bargaining relationship is defined as "any situation in which an affiliate, or any local or other subordinate body thereof, has either (a) been recognized by the employer (including any governmental agency) as the collective bargaining representative for the employees involved for a period of one year or more, or (b) been certified by the National Labor Relations Board or other federal or state agency as the collective bargaining representative for the employees." An established work relationship is defined as "any work of the kind which the members of an organization have customarily performed at a particular plant or work site whether their employer is the plant operator, a contractor, or other employer."

Affiliates are constitutionally bound by Article XXI to respect and refrain from undermining these established relationships. Presumptively, valid defenses which an aggressor union may use to justify a violation are transgression of a "basic concept of union morality," of the "constitutional objectives of the AFL-CIO," or of "accepted trade union work standards." The executive council, if it sustains such defenses by a two-thirds vote, may forgive an attack on the established relationship. However, the Article seems to protect only *established* relationships and does not appear to apply to rivalry in new organizing activities, except, perhaps, in the prohibition against "circulating or engaging in activities designed to bring another affiliate into public disrepute."

The process of resolving internal disputes, once a complaint is made, follows a five-stage sequence: (1) mediation by members of a panel from within the federation; (2) determination by an impartial umpire from outside the labor movement, selected from a pre-established panel; (3) appeal from the umpire's determination to an executive council subcommittee; (4) appeal, if granted by the subcommittee, to the whole executive council; and (5) where appeal is denied by the subcommittee, determination of the umpire is final. If, after a finding of guilt, noncompliance continues, the offending union is subject to discipline through loss of standing as a complainant in a federation proceeding, federation assistance to affiliates resisting the raid, publicizing of noncompliance, and still other penalties. Resort to court or "other legal proceedings" is expressly prohibited.[35]

This internal disputes procedure is part of a network of internal disputes mechanisms. These include the National Joint Board for Settlement of Jurisdictional Disputes in the Building and Construction Industry, administered on the union side through the Building and Construction Trades Department. Adherence to this means of settling disputes is required to maintain affiliation with the Building and Construction Trades Department. Other mechanisms are bilateral union pacts and the Organizational Disputes Agreement administered by the Industrial Union Department, which contains the most sweeping ban on inter-union conflict. This agreement applies to disputes over new organizing as well as raids on established relationships. All of these mechanisms, with the exception of the bilateral pacts, require the use of "outside" arbitrators.[36]

CHAPTER IX

Power and Influence
Within the AFL-CIO

Power and influence within the federation flow from one or more of three sources: (1) the national union base from which the bid for power is made; (2) the personal skill, style, and organization which the contender for power is able to command; and (3) the viability of the objectives for which power is sought.

MEN OF INFLUENCE

Six men have been particularly influential in the power structure of the AFL-CIO within the past decade or more. They are George Meany, Walter Reuther, James R. Hoffa, A. Philip Randolph, Arthur Goldberg, and Jay Lovestone. The first four are what might be called "political" leaders in that they hold high elective office; the other two have been labor movement professionals.

George Meany, its president, is the one most important individual in the federation.[1] The source of his power is not the national union from which he comes—the Plumbers—nor is it especially the building trades of which the Plumbers is a part, even though this has been helpful in winning acceptance for decisions distasteful to the building trades. This power is in large part the product of the great personal force exerted by an able, blunt-spoken, and decisive man who has had an uncomplicated conception of what he wants and the strong will—which not infrequently becomes willfulness—to drive it through to a conclusion.

These qualities enabled Meany to put the long-stalled unity negotiations back on the track through the simple expedient of offering to bargain with the CIO as an equal. The previous AFL position, that the CIO return to the "house of labor" before unity negotiations could begin, had proved to be an untenable condition, and since the fires of unity had not been burning brightly on either side, it was just as well. Meany subsequently bulled unity through the AFL in the face of a singular lack of enthusiasm. Meany has been the decisive influence in the federation against readmission of a Teamsters union headed by Hoffa, and in the ethical practices power of the federation. The approval of the internal disputes agreement at the 1961 convention is a Meany achievement. The "hard" and unremitting anti-communist line in international policy—from which he has not been diverted by the easing of United States and Soviet Union tensions in the post-Stalin years—also derives its main source of strength from Meany.

The contrast between Meany and his AFL predecessor, William Green, could not be more striking. For Green the federation was simply a register of national union interests; for Meany the federation has a responsibility to initiate and lead. Meany's exercise of federation leadership, allowing for differences in personal idiosyncrasies, has been in the CIO style of Lewis and Murray. Gompers was a leader, but he led by sagacity and only rarely by strength of will, as has Meany.

The other great personal figure in the AFL-CIO is Walter P. Reuther, president of the UAW, the Industrial Union Department of the federation, and, before the merger, of the CIO. He is the established leader of what is still the most dynamic national union in the American labor movement and the leader of the old CIO forces. Reuther is a product of industrial unionism, functioning in one of the strategic sectors of the economy. The high priority given to political action and public policy and to the formulation of rational bargaining programs in Reuther's scheme of unionism is directly traceable to his automobile industrial-union, mass-production environment. Reuther also has a flair for dramatizing and galvanizing action in behalf of original and wide-ranging programs. The intensity and comprehensiveness of the federation's interest in public policy owes much to Reuther's influence.

The relationship between Reuther and Meany has not always been amicable. It has been marked not only by conflicts in temperament but also by differences over policies. Reuther has been critical of failures in the federation's organizing performance, and of the federation's relationship to the international labor movement. On occasion Meany and Reuther have supported contending candidates for government posts.[2]

A third figure of importance is not now a leader of an AFL-CIO union. He is James R. Hoffa, the president of the Teamsters union,[3] whose place in the federation's power structure stems primarily from the importance of his union in the complex of inter-union relations, especially among the building trades. He is personally obnoxious to Meany, who, it is said, has set Hoffa's removal as president as the price of the Teamsters readmission to the AFL-CIO. Were it not for Meany's opposition, even a Hoffa-led Teamsters union could probably have been—at least until Hoffa's conviction on charges of jury tampering—readmitted into the AFL-CIO, although there might have been some resistance from such recent victims of Teamster raids as the CWA.

The importance of A. Philip Randolph in the federation stems not from the power of the Sleeping Car Porters union but from his role for a generation as the unrelenting and foremost critic of the labor movement's discriminatory practices against Negroes, first in the AFL and then within the AFL-CIO. Randolph's role during this period is, of course, part of the larger strategy shaping the civil rights revolution. Even though there has been a substantial improvement in the labor movement's treatment and awareness of the Negro worker, Randolph has refused to be "reasonable," jabbing the raw nerves of the federation's performance in this field on every occasion in and out of federation forums. He has, in addition, been instrumental in the formation of the Negro American Labor Council as a pressure group to prod the federation. However abrasive the criticism by Randolph and the NAACP, it has contributed to increasing federation pressure against the discriminatory practices of its affiliates. It also was influential in producing the federation's indispensable—as it turned out—lobbying for the Civil Rights Act.

Arthur Goldberg came into the national labor movement as the general counsel for the Steelworkers and the CIO. After the AFL-CIO merger, he became the general counsel for the IUD, and special counsel to the new federation, while continuing in his Steelworkers post. One of his first tasks in the CIO was to organize the ouster proceedings against the communist unions by designing an internal due process procedure consisting of a trial committee, an opportunity for examination and cross-examination of witnesses and submission of evidence at the hearing, a trial committee report, and formal action by the convention. The subsequent expulsions by the CIO marked the end of communist unionism as a national force.

Later, Goldberg shared with Meany the major responsibilities for pushing through the AFL-CIO merger. Goldberg's approach to the design of a constitutional government for the new federation was to adapt forms, processes, principles, and language from both AFL and CIO sources. The major effort was to find a common but viable ground for the federation's regulation of jurisdiction and racketeering.

Goldberg's contribution to the merger went beyond technical skill. He brought to the table his own special talents of patience, persuasion, fairness, and good sense. These were considerable contributions because, after twenty years of estrangement, the two federations were hardly capable of communicating with each other. There was in fact no universal enthusiasm for unification on either side. Only Meany and a handful of his immediate allies on the AFL side were strongly committed to unity. On the CIO side, sentiment for merger was most significantly crystallized in the person of Goldberg. After merger, with

Meany providing the political force, Goldberg became the moving figure in enforcing the ethical practices provisions. The concepts of due process proceedings, which Goldberg had established for the communist expulsions, also prevailed in the corruption trials. His accomplishments were all the more notable because they were effected while he was heavily involved in a critical period in steel industry collective bargaining and Steelworkers' union internal unrest.

Jay Lovestone personifies another sort of professional or technical role within the federation. The evolution of the AFL's international ideology, from the isolationism of the between-the-wars period to its present strong commitments, was mainly Lovestone's achievement. But Lovestone could not function without political support which was first provided in the AFL by David Dubinsky and Matthew Woll. After merger, Lovestone continued to be highly influential in the development of federation international policy. However, the intensity of CIO feeling against him prevented him from occupying a formal position commensurate with his real power until December 1963, when Walter Reuther apparently took the position, according to an observer, "that Mr. Lovestone had been the federation's international affairs director in everything but name for years anyway." [4] Since the merger, Lovestone's strength has derived from Meany's confidence in his judgment and resources. Lovestone combined strong convictions and an ideology of anti-communism with his unparalleled knowledge of and experience in the communist and anti-communist movements. He also brought a corps of able, dedicated, and experienced associates, most notably Irving Brown who has, like Lovestone, become a source of controversy in the federation and the ICFTU.

BLOCS WITHIN THE FEDERATION

The dominant blocs in the federation are the building trades and the industrial unions working through their respective departments. Although the departments are constitutionally subordinate bodies, they lead virtually independent lives, and take on other departments and at times the federation as adversaries.

The issue that gives the cutting edge to the debate between the building trades and the industrial unions is essentially a job issue. (The various facets of this issue have been discussed in part in Chapter II.) As a jurisdictional issue, the debate is over whether certain types of work—usually maintenance—shall be performed by employees working for a factory employer or by employees working for an outside subcontractor. In the former, members of the industrial union do the work; in the latter, the members of a building trades union are likely to do it. The industrial unionists have charged that the efforts of the building trades unions to secure this work, including boycotts and strikebreaking, have flagrantly transgressed the bounds of union morality. The building trades counter by asserting that the industrial unionists' criticisms have given aid and comfort to anti-union elements.

The differences between the blocs have had legislative applications in proposed amendments to the Taft-Hartley Law. The building trades had been pressing for an amendment which would legalize union picketing at multi-employer construction job sites. The IUD sought additional amendments legalizing such picketing for their unions as well, which the building trades interpreted as preventing passage of their own bill. Even the issue of discrimination has a building trades versus industrial union dimension in that the burden of the Negro discrimination charge is directed, as has been noted, against the construction unions.

It is not, however, a pure ideological craft versus industrial union battle that is being waged here, since virtually all of the building trades unions have substantial factory worker memberships and function in these situations as industrial unions. But no matter how much the construction unions have become "industrialized," there still remains a strong residue of the bitterness of anti-industrial union feeling of the thirties. Despite the fact that the former "Young Turks" of the CIO are now in their forties and fifties with records of twenty to twenty-five years of experience, the building trades leaders still look upon them as upstarts. The main onus is reserved for Walter Reuther, who has epitomized all of the radical—in the special sense in which they use the term—qualities of his breed: his interest in program, his anti-Miami asceticism, his concern with causes, and his lack of the amenities of the good companion. For the industrial unionist, the building trades leaders symbolize the "business agent" mentality which they associate with corruption and discrimination.

For its part, the IUD has sought to promote the militant spirit and the larger public objectives which gave the CIO in its prime its special quality as a social movement on the march. Thus, while the federation did not support the Civil Rights March on Washington in 1963, the IUD did.

Although the central bodies are technically subordinate to the national federation, in practice, the bodies are strong power centers in their own right. Unless they run into head-on conflict with a vital interest of the federation, these bodies experience virtually no dictation from Washington. The capacity of the state and local bodies to sustain an independent stance against the national federation was evidenced in the threats of expulsion which Meany had to use in forcing mergers on unwilling AFL and CIO city and state central bodies. In fact, merger at this level proved to be far more difficult than the merger of the national federations. In at least one state, New Jersey, the merger has been dissolved, and elements of the former CIO group have reorganized themselves into a state council of the Industrial Union Department.

The state and local central bodies represent the labor movement to their respective communities; and in almost every state and in every city of any size (irrespective of political complexion) the labor movement has an established—even if not necessarily decisive—place in the power structure. The central body is a forum to which local unions may bring contending claims, and in well-established labor communities the approval of the central body is an important asset for a union to have in a jurisdictional controversy or in an organizing drive. In many communities the backbone of the AFL central body has been the building trades unions, and the building trades versus industrial union debate has, therefore, given a sharper edge to the local merger problem.

It is at the central body level that the ouster of the Teamsters has, in many respects, been most deeply felt. Teamster aid is always helpful, if not indispensable, to the success of a strike. A Teamster was -invariably a high officer of the central body, and the size of Teamster membership made it an important financial mainstay. Despite the Teamsters' ouster, fraternization between the AFL-CIO establishment and the important Teamster elements is still an important fact in the labor movement in many areas.

CONTINUITIES AND CONTRASTS

The present federation government represents both historic continuities and contrasts. The most striking contrast with the past is the constitutional power conferred on the federation to deal with corruption, discrimination, and jurisdictional conflict in national union affiliates. It amounts to a material modification of the traditional principle of autonomy. Intervention by previous federation presidents was not uncommon, but it was based on personal prestige and not on constitutional authority. Also noteworthy in this context is labor leadership's acceptance of impartial outsiders functioning as quasi-judges in the jurisdictional disputes tribunals—a field once regarded as the labor movement's own business.

Meany uses personal influence more forthrightly than did William Green, his immediate AFL predecessor, but probably less than John L. Lewis and Philip Murray. This is not because Meany is less assertive, but because the national union affiliates are stronger than they were in the CIO of the Lewis-Murray era. The greater power of the federation is also derived from the larger numbers in the labor movement. The federation means more today because it is more.

Classical Gompers' voluntarism—the labor movement's version of laissez-faire—has been almost completely abandoned.[5] Public policy occupies a central place in the economic order, on the union's agenda, and, therefore, on the agenda of the federation of unions. Only in respect to political nonpartisanship has the federation adhered to traditional ideology, in the sense that it is formally neutral with respect to Democrats and Republicans. This neutrality, however, is more formal than real because the labor movement is, in a sense, a kind of working class party within the national Democratic Party, and within many state Democratic parties. In the present period, moreover, union nonpartisanship, such as it is, is supported by a going political concern managed by union leaders who "belong" in the circles of political power. Nothing like this existed under the older, pre-1933 nonpartisanship, and it constitutes a difference in degree which has become a difference in kind.

The abandonment of voluntarism is a change in philosophy reflecting a change in the underlying situation. Before voluntarism had become an unyielding dogma, the distrust of government intervention in economic affairs was derived from actual experience with government as a class state. Thus, it was the state of the *ex-parte* injunction, the "yellow dog" contract, and the national guard as strikebreakers. It was John L. Lewis' special genius that he recognized and acted on the possibility that the state could also be responsive to the workers as a mass political movement. In short, the state could mean Wagner acts and social security and wage-hours laws, as well as coercive power directed against unions.

Neither the AFL nor the CIO was without experience in international affairs prior to the merger. But the magnitude, organization, aggressiveness, and impact of the present federation program is a major effort instead of a casual interest. Another contrast with the historic past is the virtual disappearance of an organized radical left as a contending force either in the federation or in the larger labor movement. The American labor movement is in the unusual position of being the only national labor center of a democracy where an organized socialist or communist left, either in control or in significant opposition, is without influence.

The main historic continuity is the unchallenged primacy of the national unions in the spheres of collective bargaining and internal union management. The areas newly subject to federation regulation do not affect the national unions' control over collective bargaining. Nor do they affect the hard core of internal union administration. (The federation, of course, remains involved in collective bargaining for the dwindling number of directly affiliated unions.)

In the face of unity, diversities in union interests persist, the most persistent being craft versus industrialist. However, while there may be a lingering note of ideology, today the main differences turn on conflicting job claims conditioned by diverse job environments.

The major void in federation performance is its failure to find a viable mechanism, or possibly a strong enough will, to organize new members. Whether this is to be viewed as a failure of the federation or as the result of circumstances which the federation alone cannot alter, still remains uncertain. There is the additional question of whether a federation composed of established national unions will be permitted to supersede their interests in organizing—however ephemeral the interests of the national unions may be. The early CIO carried on organizing in its own right only in the absence of affiliates with jurisdictional claims. It is important to remember that the critical CIO effort in steel was essentially a creature of the Miners, and that in textiles of the Amalgamated Clothing Workers. Whether the national unions are prepared to let the federation stake out new organizing as an area of federation intervention—as it has in corruption, civil rights, and jurisdiction—and, if the federation were permitted to do so, whether it would make any difference, is an open question at this point.

CHAPTER X

Inside Politics
of the Union

An important and recurrent theme in this book is that union workers and leaders not only have differences with the employer but with each other. Jurisdiction is, in fact, a way of keeping differences among groups of workers within orderly bounds. Diversity in the union stems from two basic sources: one is the belief that there are not enough jobs to go around—and workers, naturally, have differences over who should get the scarce jobs; the second is that jobs in modern industry do not exist in isolation—they are related to each other. Consequently, workers differ among themselves, as well as with employers, as to how the jobs are to be related. There are other important sources of difference, among them: the role of the union in the total society; who gets what job in the union; and how much power shall the union have over its members and in relation to other union bodies.

Politics within the union reflect, express, and resolve differences among workers. By politics is meant "the activity *by which government is made possible* when differing interests in an area to be governed grow powerful enough to be conciliated." [1] It must be emphasized that

politics signifies not only differences but also their conciliation, "if government is to be made possible" by something short of total force and coercion. Politics in the union
consists of: (1) the kinds of special interests which divide
workers; (2) the organizational means which workers'
groups use to press for their special interests; (3) the
established forums and other means which are available
for the discussion and resolution of contending interests;
(4) the ways in which diverse interests are conciliated
to permit the union to function; and (5) the ways in
which diverse interests are coerced into compliance, in
contradiction to the political processes of conciliation.

SPECIAL INTERESTS

The main locale of difference among workers is the
workplace. Historically, the most persistent workplace difference has been between skilled workers or craftsmen on
the one side and production workers on the other. At the
roots of this particular difference is perhaps the craftsman's
view that the production worker, with his characteristically
small investment in acquiring skill, will undermine and
displace the skilled worker, with his characteristically large
investment in acquiring and maintaining skill. The industrial worker has felt, by contrast, that the craftsman
will protect his own special interests by weakening the
force of other worker interests.

Craft-industrial interests confront each other in many
forms.[2] One form of confrontation in the AFL-CIO has been
the division between the building trades unions and industrial unions, as has been seen. In the national unions,
the interplay of interests around the attempts of the craftsmen to recover lost ground in their positions relative to
the production workers has also been noted.[3] In the 1930's,
it was the production workers who took the offensive in the
CIO's upsurge.

Diversity based on skill interests is seen most directly
in the local union because it is closest to the job. The tire
builders in the Rubber Workers has been described as "a
strong united work group in the plant and within the
union. . . . They chose their elected officials upon the
basis of service to the tire-builders, not the union." [4] In

the Transport Workers Union of the New York City transit system, as George Taylor has reported, the "craftsmen did not think that the leadership was adequately defending their particular interests . . ." [5]

The skilled versus production worker cleavage does not exhaust the diversity of job interests. The modern industrialized enterprise, with its intricate network composed of organizational and occupational status systems, is a prolific breeding ground of difference and conflict. The union examples are many. Women members in a meatpacking local organized to oust a male president who they felt had agreed too readily to elimination of their job opportunities. In an auto local, the night shift workers provided the margin for the defeat of an incumbent officer because he called the union meetings at a time when they could not attend. In another auto local, an incumbent president was defeated because the members associated his policy with reduced earnings resulting from short-time work. In the Musicians union a large West Coast local seceded from the national union in protest against the use of record royalties to support unemployed musicians; another facet of this controversy was expressed in a conflict of interests between the full-time musicians and the casual musicians who probably make up the majority of the AFM's membership. In the West Coast Longshoremen, the "B" men, i.e., the nonpermanent employees, organized the Longshore Jobs Defense Committee "to regain its members' jobs on the San Francisco waterfront"—jobs which were reportedly eliminated by the Mechanization and Modernization Agreement negotiated between the International Longshoremen and Warehousemen's Union and the Pacific Maritime Association.[6]

Differences in perception of interest are demonstrated by the regularity with which rank-and-file members in industries affected by technological change rebel at settlements negotiated at higher union levels. Membership unrest in newspapers, automobiles, West Coast pulp and paper, longshore (East Coast), steel, and coal mining, suggests that many top level union negotiators had not at first fully grasped the depths of local concern over technology's threat to job security.[7] Perceptions of interests differ, depending on how far the parties are from the workplace. In issues involving the manpower effects of technological change, the farther away the union leader is himself from the job situation, the less stress he puts on who gets the job, as long as there is some offset of the job loss. The closer the union leadership is to the job, the more the leadership reflects rank-and-file concerns with the minute details of job shifts and job conditions, and the less it appreciates the economics of the enterprise which make changes necessary.

Shifts in the distribution of power in the union organization generate differences between those who will lose power and those who will gain power. CWA's road to national unionism from its beginnings as a loose confederation of regional associations was strewn with intense controversy and secession.[8] A major conflict issue in the AFSCME was "regionalism"—that is, "whether election of [national union] board members by region or at large is more democratic." [9] The administration favored the latter, and the district heads, who lead the opposition, favored the former. The underlying consideration was that an at-large board member has a more diffused power base than a member from a specific constituency. Both Dave Beck and James Hoffa—the latter most notably—generated opposition to their programs of centralized bargaining on the part of local and area leaders whom Hoffa styled "kings of their individual little isolated areas." [10]

Ethnic and racial considerations are major sources of diversity of interest. In recent years, the Negro worker's place in the union and in the union leadership has been the dominant interest issue of this type. The union mirrors the larger society, and it is not surprising that it has been a major battleground of the civil rights revolution. In general, wherever in the union there is ethnic or racial diversity, there are corresponding ethnic or racial interest groups.[11]

The personal style of an incumbent leader frequently provides a basis for opposition, or at least serves as a rationalization for it. In the 1965 campaign for the presidency of the United Steel Workers, the forces allied with Secretary-Treasurer Abel, as has been seen, directed their fire against President McDonald's remoteness from the rank and file, against "tuxedo" leadership—as it was put in one Abel leaflet. Disaffection at the highest levels of the Teamsters union finds its source in Hoffa's "flashes of quick temper" and his "resorting to bare fists when aroused." [12]

The interest at issue in many unions, however, is frequently not more than a difference between "ins" and "outs." In these situations the incumbent is charged with holding himself out as "the indispensable man," being "stale," being "soft on management," or "overstepping authority." The "out" candidate is represented as "putting a little more life" and "new blood in the union's administration," somebody who will tell management where to get off. Far less frequently is the "in" group charged with being "radical" in its behavior toward management by "outs" who argue for a more moderate line. [13]

Formal ideology is relatively unimportant as a source of diversity in the contemporary labor movement. The main period of ideological warfare, 1935–1950, was marked by the presence of a significant communist power in the CIO and several of its important affiliates, and in a small number of AFL affiliates. The source of conflict during this period was not the practice of communist unionism, for this was not a distinguishable form of unionism, but the use of dominated unions as propaganda auxiliaries for the Communist Party. [14] The Catholic groups and particularly the Association of Catholic Trade Unionists became deeply involved in internal union politics aimed at ousting communists from power. The Catholic groups had no affirmative trade union philosophy, their only goal being to remove the communists from power. [15] The communists' decline and fall came with the expulsion of eleven unions from the CIO in 1949 and 1950 on grounds of communist control and domination.

In the federation, Meany and Reuther are divided, not by ideology, but by emphasis on relations with the communist bloc and on the American role in ICFTU. The mass-production industrial unions are more likely to push civil rights legislation than are the craft unions, but here too the difference is in emphasis, not in fundamental position. Below the federation level, issues of broad policy are no longer an important source of division within unions.

FORMS OF INTEREST REPRESENTATION

Except for the well-known ITU party system, the political process in the union has not produced highly institutionalized forms. "Factionalism"—to use the term by which union leaders generally refer to the organized special interest groupings within the union—has the same disreputable meaning that it has historically had in politics. It generally carries "the imputation of selfish or mischievous ends or unscrupulous methods." [16] "Factionalism," Matthew Woll once noted, "tends to destroy and weaken the organization and seeks to divide the membership in general into distinctive groups. . . . It does not make for the free and democratic discussion of the rank and file." [17] "If you want to fight," David J. McDonald told a convention dissident, "you can take on the Chamber of Commerce; . . . if you want to fight, you can take on a lot of villainous politicians who seek to put the yoke of right-to-work laws on labor's neck, but don't use democratic rights to destroy the bargaining power of the union." [18]

Many national union constitutions discourage internal union politics by "regulations with regard to libel and slander that may seriously hamper, if not destroy," the expression of critical views through pamphlets and the like. Some constitutions, like those of the IBEW and the ILGWU, put substantial obstacles in the way of organized group action against an incumbent officer or administration.[19] The justifying ideology which union leadership in power uses against factionalism is that politics are irrelevant in a state of siege—as Voltaire once said about liberty[20]—and the impression which union leadership seeks to convey is that the union is permanently under siege.

If the union environment has not been conducive to the development of a two-party system, it has produced other organizational forms through which interest groupings try to be heard and to exert power. For the most part, these groupings tend to be simple, casual, and informal. The forms of political organization are of the following six broad types: (1) The "party," as in the ITU, is open, permanent, and formal.[21] (2) The "club" is also permanent but less formal and open. Thus, in one plumbers' local, Jewish members organized a "club" to protest their small share of job opportunities.[22] (3) Caucuses can be permanent or temporary, informal, and somewhat open. The Teachers union has maintained opposing "Progressive" and Classroom Teachers caucuses in the form of loose alignments of locals at convention time. The Reuther administration maintains a national caucus and regional caucuses governed by steering committees. The national caucus, which meets at the convention and is open to anybody, serves as an outlet for membership criticism and complaint. In 1959, it heard criticism by Negro delegates on the absence of a Negro on the UAW international executive board. The steering committee of the national caucus has more formal objectives, such as endorsing candidates for union office and binding members to convention action on issues, particularly dues increases.[23] (4) The work group is an important type of political organization because it constitutes a "distinctive, united, and self-conscious" unit for interest pressure at the workplace.[24] It is held together by common skill or location in the production process. The associations thus generated impart a sense of "we" as against "they." The work group need not be an organic unit of the shop or the union, although it frequently is. Characteristically, it develops leadership and weapons to give force to its interests. The term "fractional bargaining" describes the tactic of the work group which utilizes a strategic advantage to press for special terms which amount to a renegotiation of a contract provision.[25] (5) The pressure-group alliance combines local special interest groups in some multiunion organization. For example, the Association of Catholic Trade Unionists operating on a city chapter basis has been mostly concerned with organizing against communist influence. With the decline of communist power in the unions, ACTU chapters seem to have lost their reason for being. Other Catholic groups based in Jesuit labor schools have been organized against racketeering elements in unions.[26] The Negro-American Labor Council, it has been seen, is an association of Negro trade unionists in a national organization with local branches, to combat discrimination in the labor movement. Another anti-discrimination group is the Trade

Union Leadership Council in Detroit composed largely of UAW Negro leaders who successfully opposed an officially UAW-endorsed candidate for mayor of Detroit.[27] (6) The undercover organization is a more or less secret and disciplined organization. The classic example is the Communist Party cell, composed of party members within a union unit. The cell is a formal but secret organization, intended to promote Communist Party power, and to make possible control of the union by a tightly knit, highly disciplined group, subject to the direction of an external "party functionary." Also undercover, and without ideology, is the "syndicate" of racketeers in control of a union. Though not open, it seems to be permanent and formal.

FORUMS

The most common forum for discussion and resolution of contending interests is the great network of formal meetings built into the system of union government. The meetings arise out of different processes which include those of: (1) direct membership government, as in the local union and shop meetings; (2) executive and administrative authority, as in the committee and executive board meetings; (3) judicial authority, as in the sessions of hearings and appeals committees; and (4) representative government, as in the meetings of central bodies, conventions, and delegate assemblies of one kind or another.

Campaigns for elections at all levels of union government provide another regular forum for the airing of differences. Defeat of incumbent local officers is common, and of national and federation officers much less common, although recent years have witnessed the unseating of a number of national officers.[28]

Under public law, a wide range of legal forums is available to which the dissatisfied group or individual may turn for the advancement of a special interest. The established union may be displaced or confirmed as the collective bargaining representative in an NLRB representation proceeding. NLRB remedies are also available to union dissidents who claim victimization on the job because of their union activity [section 8(b)(2) and 8(a)(3)]. State courts under their general equity power and federal courts under LMRDA provide forums in which union interests in conflict may be heard and adjudicated.

When they deem the forums established by public and union law inadequate, pressure groups inside the union may resort to the direct action of the wildcat strike, the jurisdictional strike, and the slowdown. These sanctions are more commonly directed at the employer, but their tactical use to pressure the union leadership by way of the employer is well established.

POLITICS OF CONSENSUS

If differences within it are so much the order of things, how, it may be asked, does the union hold together long enough to get its business done? The first answer to this question is that, whatever other differences exist, there is no difference on the principle that the union is an appropriate instrument to protect and advance the workers' interests against the employer. The second is that politics, while a product and expression of differences, is also a method of conciliating differences so as to achieve the kind of consensus necessary to get things done. "Without consensus," it has been observed, "a political system allowing the peaceful 'play' of power, the adherence by the 'outs' to decisions made by the 'ins,' and the recognition by the 'ins' of the rights of the 'outs'—there can be no democracy." [29] The processes by which special interest groups are conciliated for a common purpose function so routinely that it has obscured for many the acute divisions that may in fact underlie the politics of consensus.

The most common approach to conciliation of special interests is to allocate the rewards available to the union according to some acceptable formula. The rewards may be in power, prestige, or recognition within the union. This calls for an equitable division among the interests of posts on union governing bodies, honorific roles at union ceremonies, opportunities to be away from the shop at conferences or conventions and to be reimbursed for "lost time" and expenses. Moving on to the higher reaches of power, the creation of a special unit in the union for the skilled trades or the professionals, or an autonomous department for a branch of the industry, may be ways of conciliating special job groups.

In collective bargaining, conciliation means rationing the gains so that the package finally negotiated incorporates, for instance, a cash wage increase for the younger men, an improvement in pensions for the older men, an increase in shift differentials for the second and third shifts, an above-average increase for the skilled workers to maintain their customary wage differential, and an improvement in the maternity allowance for the women employees.

ANTI-POLITICS AND UNION ABSOLUTISM

The contradiction of politics is the achievement of order through coercion, rather than through the political method of shared power and recognition among the differing interests. In the union, absolute power is enforced by manipulating its internal processes and by coercion on the job.

The strategic points at which union government is susceptible to manipulation are the union meetings, conventions, elections, trusteeships, and disciplinary procedures. Attempts to manipulate meetings and conventions are usually made in the interests of an incumbent leadership, but it is not rare for a determined and well-disciplined outgroup to disorganize meetings through heckling, parliamentary maneuver, and/or violence.[30] The holding of conventions has in instances been postponed "legally" for as long as twelve years, as in the case of the Operating Engineers, and for thirty years in the Laborers.[31] Trusteeships have been used by national union leaders to oust hostile local leaders and to control the votes of a local's convention delegates. Elections have been stolen or fixed by stuffing ballot boxes, miscounting, or by disenfranchising local groups. The disciplinary procedure has been used for control purposes by applying vague grounds like "conduct unbecoming a union member" or "promoting unrest" to critics of the incumbent leadership.[32]

Job coercion assumes two basic forms. In one the business agent gets the employer to fire "troublemakers" in the local; in the other the workers in a factory situation, with or without suggestion, make life at work unbearable for strikebreakers, public advocates of "right-to-work" laws, or supporters of rival unions. The former is illegal under the Taft-Hartley Law [section 8b(2) and 8a(3)], and is characteristically found in the building trades situations.[33] In aggravated cases of union absolutism, particularly of the racketeering variety, violence against the leaders of opposition groups is not uncommon.[34]

If the political process is something in which "an active and legitimate group can make itself heard effectively at some crucial stage in a decision,"[35] then the evidence is that, despite occasional deviations, politics is the rule in the union and, indeed, is of the essence of unionism. "A trade union is a political agency operating in an economic environment."[36]

CHAPTER XI

The Union as a Government—
A Summing-Up

The union represents an institutionalization of workers' deeply-rooted reactions to the disciplines and insecurities of industrialism. In fact, many of the workers' reactions, like apprenticeship and output limitation, antedate industrialism. The union as a special case of worker defense emerged at that point in economic development when, as the Webbs put it, there was "definite separation between the functions of the capitalist entrepreneur and the manual worker—between, that is to say, the direction of industrial operations and their execution." [1]

Workers do not always channel their resistance to efficiency through unions but, when they do, the union defenses are quite distinct from others they might try. The union is first a formal organization with highly structured relationships, both to its constituents, based on a constitution, and to its employers, based on a collective agreement. Second, the union's influence goes beyond the workplace. For this purpose it combines with other unions to build a labor *movement*. The national union and intermediate body have their origins in this joining together of unions to adapt their power in the labor market to that of their counterpart employers. In addition, the city, state, and national federations use their combinations of unions for legislative and political objectives.

The ascendancy of collective bargaining as the primary union function established the national union as the decisive unit in the network of union government. As a corollary, the forms of union government most adaptable to politics and legislation (the city, the state, or the national federation) were relegated to secondary positions. After President Roosevelt's election, the union's interest in politics and legislation became stronger and with this growing interest there was a decided renewal of federation power. But at no time has the preeminence of collective bargaining been in any way impaired.

The organizational form which unionism takes is that of a government with written constitutions, government organs to carry out the purposes of the constitution, effective sanctions to enforce compliance with the orders of the government, "due process" standards to protect against arbitrary use of sanctions and, finally, physical existence as a government. The constitutions vest sovereignty in a popular constituency, either directly, through a referendum or mass meeting, or indirectly, through a delegate assembly. The constitutions also set out the objectives, organs, and functions of the government, and lay claim to a territory or jurisdiction. While the constitution is largely concerned with regulating the relationships within the union, the collective agreement—which is another sort of constitution—regulates the employment relationship between the union and the employer. Over this relationship, by virtue of the collective agreement and by civil law, the union has exclusive authority in the appropriate unit of jurisdiction.

The organs of the union government carry on two broad functions: collective bargaining and internal administration. For many unions, legislative and political activity is emerging as a third major function. A few unions also engage in business enterprise, most commonly but not limited to mutual insurance.

The union is constitutionally empowered to employ a variety of means to enforce compliance with its decisions and rules. Against members, the union may impose penalties up to and including expulsion—which is frequently tantamount to a denial of employment in a particular trade or industry. Against subordinate branches, the superior union body may suspend, expel, or take over the organization. Against the employer, the union may withhold the labor of its constituents by way of a strike. However, the power of the union government to enforce these sanctions is limited by "due process" standards set out in its own constitution, in the civil law, or in the collective agreement.

The union government has a real existence. There are offices and employees who function in union halls and buildings, members who pay dues and come to meetings where agreements are formulated and ratified, strikes are authorized, and political candidates and programs are debated.

LIMITATIONS OF UNION AS GOVERNMENT

Nevertheless, when compared to the civil government, the union falls short of being a complete government. The union is first of all a special purpose government: its effective power is limited to the worker's employment relationship. Moreover, the means by which the union secures itself against membership attrition—exclusive representation, union shop, and the check-off—are all exercised by dispensation from the civil government. A representation election directed by the civil government in an employee unit determined by that government may even jeopardize the very existence of the union—by exposing it to displacement by a rival union or by no union. There are, in any case, many more non-union job territories than union territories, since only a minority of the labor force is represented by unions. But the union's presence may influence conditions in the non-union sector.

Union constitutions do not fully reflect the scope and function of union government. Nor do the working people who man these governments hold to the view that every union action must find its legitimacy in a constitutional provision. Frequently the leaders go beyond the democratic requirements of the constitution rather than short-circuiting it, as for example, in seeking membership approval for a strike or a new contract.

To summarize: The union undoubtedly has the major attributes of a government although its power to function like one is (a) conditional—because acquiescence by the civil government, the employer, and by the employees in the unit is essential for its functions; (b) partial—because it is applicable only to a segment of its potential constituency; (c) restricted—since the employment interests of its constituency represent the boundary of its effective control; (d) expendable or replaceable—because the employer may keep the union out by simulating union conditions, or a rival union may win out; (e) pragmatically oriented— since the test is more of what needs to be done than of whether an action is formally proper under union law.

THE PRINCIPLES OF UNION GOVERNMENT

The union governmental units relate to each other in such a way that the federation is primarily a voluntary association of national unions, and that the national union is primarily an association of subordinate intermediate bodies, locals, and shop units. From the founding of the AFL the federation has been viewed as an association of national unions operating on a limited grant of power by the affiliated national unions who *are* the federation. Thus the AFL-CIO stands formally in the relationship of a federation to the national unions because "the powers of the central or federal authority are limited by certain powers secured to the units which have united for common purposes." [2] The ultimate counter-sanction secured to the national union is its unquestioned right to secede from the federation.

The national union occupies the decisive place in the governmental scheme because it controls the collective bargaining function which is the mainspring of all union influence. The local and intermediate unions, in the constitutional theory of the American labor movement, are each an instrumentality of the national union and each exercises authority under conditions prescribed by the national union constitution. The national union is a "unitary" authority in the sense that the powers possessed by the subordinate bodies are, in theory, held at the discretion of the national union.[3] In practice, this national union authority is only as good as is its capability to enforce this authority against secession or rival movements in the subordinate body. In cases where the subordinate body operates in a local market environment it necessarily acts with an independence more consistent with a federal than a unitary relationship.

Politics is the essence of union dynamics. The source of politics is the interplay of interests generated by diversity in jobs, ethnic attachments, status, and ideology. The political strain so permeates the fabric of union government that it has undoubtedly stunted the growth of the kind of classical bureaucracy which derives its strategic position from "specialization, a hierarchy of authority, a system of rules, and impersonality." [4] Its closest approximations to bureaucracy are the two categories of union staff—the "servicing" type of union representative, and the professional or technical staff. The former, whatever other qualifications he needs, must as a condition of employment be politically acceptable to his principals. His technical competence counts more with the professional staff member, but even he must conform to important political specifications as a condition of hire and continued employment. This professional, who most closely resembles the classical bureaucrat, is numerically inconsequential in the union. When, as occasionally happens, a technician or professional does rise to policy-making power, this is more as a consequence of personal qualities than of an inherent bureaucratic advantage.

This failure of a classical bureaucracy to develop is due, in the main, to the failure of an objective science of union administration to gain acceptance. (In striking contrast is the evolution of a scientific management, which has been a major force for bureaucracy on the enterprise side.) Every issue in collective bargaining and in internal union government cuts across vital interests and is therefore infused with a political essence which defies the objectivity of bureaucracy. The union leader who has grown up in this politically loaded environment will not easily accept the domination of a professional technician—who is by definition presumably beyond politics. The only kinds of professional skill which most union leaders accept as functionally necessary are accounting, law, and medicine. These are necessary, in their view, to comply with the law of the civil government, or because the skills are admittedly beyond their own capacities. Most union leaders would not be prepared to make this latter concession for the professional in journalism, education, or research. In addition, the large social and educational distance between them makes even more unlikely the subordination of the political trade union leader to the union professional.

THE UNION AS A DEMOCRACY

The union is judged not only by whether it performs its functions effectively but also by whether it performs them democratically. To this end one must define democracy in a manner relevant to the union's legitimate purposes and needs. The present approach is a definition in terms of four operational elements of democracy in unionism. The elements (borrowing liberally from general theorists of democracy) are: (1) the pervasiveness of democratic *rule;* that is, the extent to which the popular constituency actually engages in the processes of direct government of the shop and the local union;[5] (2) the pervasiveness of popular *control* if popular *rule* would render legitimate union purposes impractical; popular control means "the availability of various processes by which the government is kept responsible" [6] to the underlying membership in the representative or delegate forms of union government as in the large locals, intermediate bodies and national unions; (3) the presence of a continuous active political process, that is, "one in which an active and legitimate group in the population can make itself heard effectively at some crucial stage in the process of decision." Effectiveness turns on whether or not "officials . . . expect to suffer in some significant way [including loss of office] if they do not placate the group, its leaders, or its most vociferous members";[7] (4) the right to criticize and campaign against the union leadership, without fear of reprisal.

By these criteria, the general run of local unions are viable democratic governments, especially in respect to collective bargaining. There is, in fact, direct rule in the local union and its substructure on the important issues;

an active and continuous political process including replacement of leadership; and a largely uninhibited and open criticism of the union performance. Of course, there are also exceptions and qualifications. For the factory local union, the chances are that the general agreement is negotiated by a supralocal body. But this does not impair the integral role that the local union takes in the enforcement of that agreement, in the direct negotiation of local practices, and in the decision processes of the supralocal bodies. In the non-factory local, the business agent may not always be effectively subject to democratic rule or control.

Popular control and politics in collective bargaining are real in the national union. There is extensive local participation in the various processes, including bargaining conferences, strike votes, and contract ratification votes; and there is considerable local supplementation and enforcement of national bargaining, all of which acts to make this popular control effective. However, the national union's internal administration—unlike its collective bargaining processes—suffers from several deficiencies in democracy, specifically: the large area of unreviewable power exercised by the president; the failure of the executive board, and in turn of the convention, to serve as checks on the executive authority; the use of the union periodical as an instrument of the administration in power; and the failure of the constitution to reflect the full range of union functions.

Several national unions seem recently to have entered a new period of democratic and political vitality. Powerful national union presidents or their chosen replacements have been defeated; if not defeated, national union incumbents have been shaken by widespread protest and, in one important instance, by a successful secession; nationally negotiated settlements have either been rejected or their approval delayed by rank-and-file votes. Where the will is strong enough, apparently it is still possible to defeat an incumbent and even a well-entrenched leadership in the national union.

One issue of democracy in the federation is whether the federation has impaired the national union's authority in collective bargaining and internal administration. With respect to collective bargaining the national union is still supreme. The federation does indeed exercise power over the national union's internal government but with respect to dealings with corruption and civil rights in the union, and this is not incompatible with a democratic labor movement. Ultimately, a national union which considers that a vital interest has been impaired by a federation act can and will disaffiliate.

There may be a question of democracy in whether the federation's efforts to minimize interunion rivalry has reduced the rank-and-file workers' freedom to change unions. Can essential reforms be made within the union if the union is not exposed to the threat of competition? [8] On the facts: The various no-raiding agreements have not eliminated rival union contests, although the largest proportion of these contests are between AFL-CIO affiliates and unaffiliated unions.[9] One of the available case investigations of rival unionism concluded that rival unionism was "wasteful [and an] inefficient utilization of resources, and afford[ed] management important tactical advantages in collective bargaining." [10]

The political process in the AFL-CIO operates significantly: in conflicts over jurisdiction and representation, in the determination of the international policies of the federation, and occasionally in the filling of executive council vacancies. In respect to international policy, President Meany has tended to take important steps on his own authority, and to seek approval and vindication later. The council, if not the president, effectively fills its own vacancies and is subject only to a ratifying vote by the convention. Since the federation is an association of unions rather than an individual membership association, its politics function on a leader-to-leader level, not on a leader-to-member level.

Union democracy does not depend solely on the internal processes of unionism. Under federal law and the laws of thirteen states, a majority of the employees in a unit can displace or replace a collective bargaining representative.[11] The unions within the jurisdiction of LMRDA are subject to that law's provisions on membership rights, officers' disclosure, election of officers, and trusteeships. Even before LMRDA, state courts have exercised broad equity powers to deal with specific allegations of violations of members' rights.

THE EFFECT OF COLLECTIVE BARGAINING

The main determinant of union government has been the primacy of collective bargaining. The decision for collective bargaining enforced a logic and rationalization of its own on the supporting structure, government, and politics of American unions. The logic of collective bargaining has meant union structure responsive both to market forces and sectional job interests, a program of financing and administration to maintain a continuous organization durable in adversity, and a discipline in the essential routines of collective bargaining administration.

Collective bargaining has a built-in test; the union practitioner's performance can always be judged by concrete results. This instills in him a compromising, prudent, and trial-and-error attitude. As to union strategy, collective bargaining requires a middle ground between the militancy necessary for struggle and the common purpose with management necessary to maintain a viable enterprise capable of producing gains for the workers.

By contrast, a union for which a social reform movement was primary would require other instrumentalities and temperaments. Lenin captured the essence of this problem. Preoccupied with making a revolution, Lenin preferred the union leader as a "tribune of the people" rather than as a "trade union secretary." The trade union secretary "engaged more in calling the masses to concrete actions" while the tribune expounded "the revolutionary explanation of the whole of modern society or various manifestations of it." [12]

Almost every union goes through an early phase of development when its leaders function as tribunes of the people. If the unions ultimately opt for collective bargaining, and this is what the American unions have done, then the tribune necessarily undergoes a mutation into secretary. Of the two, the secretary has greater survival value.

The American option for collective bargaining was a choice controlled in large degree by the nature of the American situation. First, a long-run scarcity of labor enhanced the unions' bargaining power. Second, unlike the labor movements of other countries, the energies of American unions were not consumed by overriding involvements in the social and political struggles for working-class citizenship and representation, for civil liberties, education, nationalism, and anti-imperialism. To be sure, the American labor movement has experienced its own consuming struggle in the battle for the right of collective bargaining. The effect of that struggle, however, was to confirm the unions still further in their view that legitimacy for collective bargaining could be achieved only by a policy of limiting their unions' social objectives. When it seemed, after Roosevelt, that a policy of self-denial in social goals had probably gone too far the other way, the labor movement reversed itself and broadened its interest in legislative enactment—but without altering the first priority assigned to collective bargaining.

The young Walter Lippmann saw very clearly how effectiveness in "the deliberate tactics" of collective bargaining may temper the mood of rebellion against the social order:

> American workers [Lippmann was talking specifically about the railroad unions] have won the very things the lack of which makes rebellion necessary. For if men are ground down in poverty, if the rights of assemblage and free speech are denied them, if their protests are ineffective and despised, then rebellion is the only possible way out. But when there is something like a democracy where wrong is not a matter of life and death, but of better and worse, then the preliminaries of civilization have been achieved, and more deliberate tactics become possible.[13]

"Business unionism" represents the organizational adaptation to the needs of collective bargaining. The distinguishing quality of business unionism in the United States is the business-like way with which American unions have gone about ordering their affairs. While their degree of rational organization and efficiency is nothing like business enterprise efficiency, nevertheless the American unions —as also the northern European unions—by their adaptation to collective bargaining functions, constitute a special class among the unions of the world.

Paradoxically, American business-like unionism has developed in tandem with an unprecedented level of union penetration into the employment functions of the business enterprise. This participation, unrivaled by any other collective bargaining system, occurs right at the plant. The paradox consists of an ideologically *pro-capitalist, business-like* unionism effectively sharing power with management in the employment function, while the ideologically *anti-capitalist, pro-socialist* unions of the world seem capable of only very limited participation in actual employment decisions.

FACTORS IN DIVERSITY

Some of the principal variations in union government are differences in: (1) the level of government; (2) the workplace environment; and (3) the stage of union development. At the grass roots level, shop and local union governments tend to be "of the most rudimentary type." [14] The rank-and-file member is socially and physically close to the union. At union meetings "one outspoken critic is often enough to hold officials to account and to prevent them from abusing their power." [15] Much of the union's business is carried on by informal face-to-face relationships, while *ad hoc* arrangements to by-pass formal procedures are not uncommon. Most of the issues that confront and concern these local groups are very close to the job, and to personal relationships on the job and in the local union.

On the higher rungs of union government the process becomes more formal, the interpersonal relationships are more leader-to-leader than member-to-leader. There is, however, an essential egalitarianism at all levels of union government under almost all circumstances which the union leader, no matter how important, violates at his peril. The issues at the higher levels are not as intensely personal and as job-site centered as in the local units. But the union is, in any case, small-scale as organizations go; and small matters are likely to occupy many of the leaders even at the highest levels. Only at the federation level and in the large national unions are the concerns of the leaders likely to be broad policy matters.

The character of union government is influenced by whether the union is in factory or non-factory employment, or relatedly by whether the union is composed of craftsmen or of industrial workers. In craft unions, most notably in the construction unions, the workplace government is very simple and almost non-existent; the important issues are really decided in the union hall. The craft unionism of the printing trades represents a more elaborate workplace government but the site of power is still the union hall.

In the craft unions important decisions are more likely to be made by local governments, and in the factory unions by the national governments. This is another way of saying that craft unions tend to be tied to local markets and factory unions to national markets. In the larger metropolitan areas, as the scope of the local market expands, the weight of power in the craft unions seems to move toward intermediate union forms.

The local craft union is likely to have decisive power centered in a paid business agent. Power in the industrial factory union is less likely to be concentrated in one leader than to be diffused through a local executive board or a plant-centered bargaining committee. The powerful and creative leaders in the industrial unions are, by this fact, more likely to be found in the upper governmental reaches; the powerful and creative leaders in the craft groups are more likely to be found in the local groups.

The degree of formality in the union government depends largely on its stage of organizational development. In the union's early life its public sees the union as a movement and fellowship and, depending on employer opposition, as an army under siege. The union in this phase is not much on formality. Its processes are carried on in the spirit of "complete, comradely, mutual confidence" among unionists.[16] Once the union's struggle for survival is over, and it confronts the need to function effectively in collective bargaining, it must evolve from fellowship to government. There is a slow, tortured, and painful process of grappling to replace "mutual confidence" with orderly and formal democratic procedures. Sometimes the union does not complete the transition under its own power and has to be forced by external authority—which may represent the current phase in the development of union government. In this phase, the civil law is superimposing on the union law a scheme of constitutional guarantees directed toward: (1) protecting membership rights; (2) prescribing standards of officer accountability and fiduciary responsibility; (3) equalizing the standing of the "ins" and the "outs" in campaigns for union office; (4) establishing safeguards for fair elections; and (5) regulating the national union's suspension of local self-government.

This work has been concerned primarily with the union as a government—with the processes of interaction between those who rule and those who are ruled. The union has other organizational faces, depending on the standpoint of the viewer. The union is a "public utility" whose behavior in internal government and collective bargaining is subject to regulation in the public interest; it is a "firm" or "organization" which seeks to maximize something in the employment transaction. The national union is seen by some as an economic "monopoly"—which like other monopolies ought to be forced to divest itself of some of its subordinate union components. To some the trade union is the "re-creation of the community" of workers atomized by economic individualism.[17] A few unions are "guilds" because, like the classic guilds, they include masters as well as apprentices and journeymen. For some, the union is or ought to be a cause, mission, or social movement aimed at fundamental reconstruction of the social order; and for those at the other pole, the union is a predatory band, levying tribute on its members and employers.

EVALUATION

Workers have woven an intricate and resourceful complex of government to improve their conditions at work and—exemplifying the great capacity of people to govern themselves—this vast network evolved from the workers' own experiences: trial and error, a history of defeats and successes and retreats, and, not least of all, from the workers' own power. There were no Montesquieus, Tocquevilles, Bryces, or Lockes to guide their steps. There was no *Federalist Paper Number 10*. These "unlettered statesmen of the Trade Union world," [18] as the Webbs called them, had only their good sense derived from struggle and their insights and values as free citizens of a free society to guide them.

Social reconstruction of a significant kind has taken place through collective bargaining but, because it has not been cast in the conventional categories of reform, its impact has been only dimly understood. The unconventional revolution made by American unions has created —to replace the unilateral administration of enterprise's employment—a system of bilateral, constitutional government in industry through collective bargaining based on membership support. To put it another way, constitutional government and the rule of law have replaced "employment by a crook of the finger at the factory gate or the toss of the brass check on the waterfront . . . huddle-fuddle and favoritism, the intolerant and sometimes contemptuous brush-off . . . and dictatorship and autocratic paternalism." [19]

In internal self-government, the union's special quality has been the uncommon ingenuity shown in shaping form to function. Beyond this, the democracy of the larger society has been strengthened by the union's acting as a laboratory for working people to acquire experience and confidence in their capacity to participate in the civil government and hence to diffuse the sources of social power.

There can be no question that for what the union set out to do, it represents "a very remarkable creative achievement" [20] which has revitalized American democracy, is indispensable to it, and could have been nurtured only in a free society.

NOTES

CHAPTER I—*Introduction*

1. The line of analysis in this section has been treated in more detail in my "The Elements of Industrial Relations," *British Journal of Industrial Relations*, London, March 1964. *See also* Abraham J. Siegel, "Method and Substance in Theorizing about Worker Protest," *Aspects of Labor Economics*, A Conference of the Universities, National Bureau Committee for Economic Research (Princeton: Princeton U. Press, 1962).

2. N. R. Whitney, *Jurisdiction in American Building-Trades Unions*, Studies in Historical and Political Science, Vol. 32 (Baltimore: Johns Hopkins Press, 1914), p. 9.

CHAPTER II—*Jurisdiction and Structure of American Unions*

1. Jack G. Day, "Jurisdiction," in U.S. Dept. of Labor, Bureau of Labor Statistics Bull. No. 1009, *Problems and Policies of Dispute Settlement and Wage Stabilization During World War II* (Washington: G.P.O., 1950).

2. N. R. Whitney, *Jurisdiction in American Building-Trades Unions*, Studies in Historical and Political Science, Vol. 32 (Baltimore: Johns Hopkins Press, 1914), p. 9.

3. Selig Perlman, *A Theory of the Labor Movement* (New York: Augustus M. Kelley, 1949 impression), pp. 239ff.

4. Sidney and Beatrice Webb, *Industrial Democracy*, Vol. II (London: Longmans, Green, 1897), pp. 563ff.

5. See any general history on the issue of structure in the development of the American labor movement. The best is Philip Taft, *Organized Labor in American History* (New York: Harper and Row, 1964).

6. See this chapter and Chapter VIII.

7. National Industrial Conference Board (NICB), *Sourcebook of Union Government, Structure and Procedures* (New York: NICB, 1956), p. 15.

8. *Ibid.,* p. 307.

9. *Ibid.,* pp. 47–48.

10. *Ibid.,* p. 72.

11. *Ibid.,* p. 79.

12. *Ibid.,* p. 190.

13. *Ibid.,* p. 24.

14. *Ibid.,* p. 277.

15. Arthur B. Shostak, *America's Forgotten Labor Organization: A Survey of the Role of the Single-Firm Independent Union in American Industry* (Princeton: Princeton U. Press, Industrial Relations Section, 1962); U.S. Dept. of Labor, Bureau of Labor-Management Reports, *Register of Reporting Labor Organizations, June 30, 1960* (Washington: G.P.O., 1960).

16. International Typographical Union, *Typographical Journal*, September 1955, p. 248.

17. Helen Wood, "Trends in the Specialization of Occupational Requirements," in William Haber *et al.*, eds., *Manpower in the United States*, Industrial Relations Research Association (IRRA), (New York: Harper and Row, 1954), p. 103; *see also* George H. Hildebrand, "External Influence and the Determination of the Wage Structure," in J. L. Meij, ed., *Internal Wage Structure* (Amsterdam: North-Holland Pub. Co., 1963); Lloyd Ulman, *The Rise of the National Trade Union* (Cambridge: Harvard U. Press, 1955), p. 308; Herbert Lahne, "The Welder's Search for Craft Recognition," *Industrial and Labor Relations Review*, July 1958, pp. 591–607.

18. H. A. Turner, *Trade Union Growth, Structure and Policy* (Toronto: U. of Toronto Press, 1962), p. 114.

19. Hildebrand, *op. cit.*, p. 267.

20. Charles J. Dempwolf, *Trade Union Organizing on the District and Local Level: A Case Study* (unpublished M.A. thesis), Rutgers U., 1956, pp. 102ff.

21. International Ladies' Garment Workers' Union, *Structure and Functioning of the ILGWU* (New York: ILGWU, 1959), p. 8.

22. "Local Unions According to States," *The Ironworker* (Publication of the International Association of Bridge, Structural and Ornamental Iron Workers), St. Louis, November 1956.

23. U.S. Department of Labor, *Manpower Utilization: Job Security in the Longshore Industry, Port of New Orleans,* Report and Findings (Washington: G.P.O., 1964).

24. U.S. Congress, Senate, Select Committee on Improper Activities in the Labor or Management Field (McClellan Comm.), *Investigation of Improper Activities in the Labor or Management Field,* Part 20 (Washington: G.P.O., 1958), p. 7924.

25. *Ibid.,* Part 19, p. 7514.

26. *The Milwaukee Journal,* May 25, 1958.

27. John T. Dunlop, "The Industrial Relations System in Construction," in Arnold Weber, ed., *Structure of Collective Bargaining* (New York: Free Press of Glencoe, 1961), p. 271.

28. Dempwolf, *op. cit.,* pp. 102ff.

29. Elmo P. Hohman, "Maritime Labor Economics as a Determinant of the Structure and Policy of Seamen's Unions," *Proceedings,* IRRA, September 1957 (Madison: IRRA, 1958), pp. 163–170.

30. See Chapter V on intermediate bodies.

31. Robert D. Papkin, "Craft Unit vs. Industrial Unit Bargaining Under the National Labor Relations Act," *George Washington Law Review,* December 1960; "Bargaining Unit Rules," *Labor Relations Expediter* (Washington Bureau of National Affairs, 1964); and an unpublished collection of teaching materials prepared and generously made available to me by Professor Thomas Holland of the George Washington University (1964).

32. National Mediation Board, *Fifteen Years Under the Railway Labor Act, 1934–1949* (Washington: G.P.O., 1950), p. 17.

33. Neil Chamberlain, "Determinants of Collective Bargaining Structures," in Weber, ed., *op. cit.,* p. 9.

34. Dunlop, in Weber, ed., *op. cit.,* p. 261.

35. John T. Dunlop, "Structural Changes in the Labor Movement and Industrial Relations System," *Proceedings*, IRRA, 1956 (Madison: IRRA, 1956), p. 23.

36. National Labor Relations Board, *28th Annual Report, Fiscal Year 1963* (Washington: G.P.O., 1964), p. 51.

37. Douglass V. Brown and George P. Shultz, "Public Policy and the Structure of Collective Bargaining," in Weber, ed., *op. cit.*, p. 318 (emphasis in original).

38. Dunlop, in Weber, ed., *op. cit.*, p. 274.

39. Chamberlain, in Weber, ed., *op. cit.*, p. 16.

40. *Ibid.*, p. 26.

41. Ralph Helstein, "Collective Bargaining in the Meat Packing Industry" in Weber, ed., *op. cit.*, p. 156.

42. Peter Henle, "Union Policy and Size of Bargaining Unit," in Weber, ed., *op. cit.*, p. 116.

43. Harold W. Davey, *Contemporary Collective Bargaining* (Englewood Cliffs: Prentice-Hall, 1959), pp. 84ff.

44. Herman Cooper, "Craft vs. Industrial Unionism," *Sixth Annual Conference on Labor* (Albany: Bender, 1953).

45. U.S. Dept. of Labor, Bureau of Labor Statistics, *Directory of National and International Unions in the United States, 1963* (Washington: G.P.O., 1963), pp. 73–74.

46. Neil Chamberlain, "The Structure of Bargaining Units," *Industrial and Labor Relations Review*, October 1956, pp. 22ff.

47. Dunlop, in Weber, ed., *op. cit.*, p. 28.

48. E. Robert Livernash, "Recent Developments in Bargaining Structure," in Weber, ed., *op. cit.*, p. 35.

49. Lloyd Ulman, *The Government of the Steel Workers Union* (Englewood Cliffs: Prentice-Hall, 1959), pp. 78–80.

50. E. Robert Livernash, *Collective Bargaining in the Steel Industry*, U.S. Dept. of Labor (Washington: G.P.O., 1960), p. 123 (emphasis my own).

51. Davey, *op. cit.*, p. 343.

52. See pp. 128–29.

53. Arnold Weber, "Craft Representation in Industrial Unions," *Proceedings*, IRRA, 1961 (Madison: IRRA, 1961); Muriel Beach, "The Problems of the Skilled Worker in an Industrial Union: A Case Study," *IL Research*, N.Y. State School of Industrial and Labor Relations, Fall–Winter 1960–1961.

54. Van Dusen Kennedy, *Nonfactory Unionism and Labor Relations* (Berkeley: U. of California Press, 1955); Hildebrand, *op. cit.; see also* my "The Rise of Industrial Unionism," William Haber, ed., *Labor in a Changing America* (New York: Basic Books, 1966).

55. Sidney and Beatrice Webb, *op. cit.*, Vol. I, p. 139.

56. National Labor Relations Board, *14th Annual Report* (Washington: G.P.O., 1949), p. 33; and *15th Annual Report* (Washington: G.P.O., 1950), pp. 41–42.

56a. Robert F. Hoxie, *Trade Unionism in the United States* (New York: Appleton-Century-Crofts, 1923), p. 88.

57. Selig Perlman, "Upheaval and Reorganization" in John R. Commons, ed., *History of Labour in the United States*, Vol. II (New York: Macmillan, 1918), pp. 533–535 *passim*.

58. John P. Frey, *Craft Unionism of Ancient and Modern Times* (Washington: John P. Frey, 1945); Julia Johnsen, *Industrial vs. Craft Unionism* (New York: H.W. Wilson, 1937). The latter is the best collection of views on the issue.

59. "Industrial Unionism," *Journal of Political Economy*, February 1935, quoted *ibid.*, p. 149.

60. See, for example, Donald A. Crawford, "Contracting Out" in George W. Taylor and Edward B. Shils, eds., *Industrial Relations in the 1960's—Problems and Prospects*, Vol. II (Philadelphia: U. of Pennsylvania Press, 1959).

61. National Labor Relations Board, *In the Matter of American Potash and Chemical Corporation, Brief Amicus Curiae*, Manufacturing Chemists Association (1953).

62. *Brief Amicus Curiae*, National Association of Manufacturers, *loc. cit.; see also* Bureau of National Affairs, *Daily Labor Report*, Special Supplement No. 19, October 7, 1953, p. 29.

63. Brown and Shultz, in Weber, ed., *op. cit.*

64. Weber, ed., *Structure of Collective Bargaining, loc. cit.*, provides a variety of representative viewpoints.

CHAPTER III—*The Local Union*

1. David J. Saposs, "Colonial and Federal Beginnings," in John R. Commons, *History of Labour in the United States*, Vol. I (New York: Macmillan, 1918), p. 107; on the local union see Leonard R. Sayles and George Strauss, *The Local Union: Its Place in the Industrial Plant* (New

York: Harper and Row, 1953); Arnold S. Tannenbaum and Robert L. Kahn, *Participation in Union Locals* (Evanston: Row, Peterson, 1958); Joel Seidman *et al.*, *The Worker Views His Union* (Chicago: U. of Chicago Press, 1958); William M. Leiserson, *American Trade Union Democracy* (New York: Columbia U. Press, 1959).

2. John R. Commons, "American Shoemakers, 1648–1895" in *Labor and Administration* (New York: Macmillan, 1923), pp. 219–66.

3. Sidney and Beatrice Webb, *The History of Trade Unionism* (London: Longmans, Green, 1920), p. 1.

4. Saposs, *op. cit.*, p. 11.

5. Norman J. Ware, *Labor in Modern Industrial Society* (Boston: Heath, 1935), pp. 134ff.

6. *Ibid.*

7. Sometimes referred to as Landrum-Griffin after the two main sponsors.

8. U.S. Dept. of Labor, Labor-Management Services Administration (LMSA), *Union Constitutions and the Election of Union Officers* (Washington: G.P.O., 1965).

9. This composite account is derived basically from the following sources: Jack Barbash, *Labor's Grass Roots* (New York: Harper and Row, 1961), Chapter III and the sources cited therein; U.S. Dept. of Labor, Bureau of Labor Statistics, Bull. No. 1350, *Disciplinary Powers and Procedures in Union Constitutions* (Washington: G.P.O., 1963); LMSA, *Union Constitutions, loc. cit.*

10. BLS, *Disciplinary Powers and Procedures, loc. cit.*, p. 1.

11. *Ibid.*, pp. 115ff.

12. The full citation is the Labor-Management Reporting and Disclosure Act, 73 Stat. 519.

13. Archibald Cox, *Law and the National Labor Policy* (Los Angeles: U. of California Press, 1960), pp. 92–93.

14. See Benjamin Aaron, "Internal Relations Between Unions and Their Members in the United States," *Rutgers Law Review*, Winter 1964, p. 288; *see also* R. W. Rideout, *The Right to Membership of a Trade Union* (London: Athlone Press, U. of London, 1963).

15. U.S. Dept. of Labor, Bureau of Labor-Management Reports (BLMR), *Report, Fiscal Year 1960* (Washington: G.P.O., 1960), pp. 25ff.

16. Cox, *op. cit.*, pp. 92–93.

17. Aaron, *op. cit.*, pp. 299–300; Joseph R. Grodin,

Union Government and the Law (Los Angeles: U. of California Press, 1961), p. 155.

18. Herbert S. Parnes, *Union Strike Votes* (Princeton: Princeton U., Industrial Relations Section, 1956), p. 67; *see also* George Strauss and Don Willner, *Government Regulation of Local Union Democracy,* in *Labor Law Journal,* N.Y. State School of Industrial and Labor Relations, Reprint Series, No. 18, August 1953.

19. The standard work on this subject of Negroes and unions is Ray Marshall, *The Negro and Organized Labor* (New York: Wiley, 1965).

20. *Ibid.,* p. 110.

21. See pp. 111 and 118 for additional discussion.

22. Marshall, *op. cit.,* pp. 237–238.

23. *Business Week,* March 14, 1961, p. 121.

24. Herbert J. Lahne, "The Union Work Permit," *Political Science Quarterly,* September 1951.

25. See Kenneth M. McCaffree, "Union Membership Policies and Labor Productivity among Asbestos Workers," *Industrial and Labor Relations Review,* January 1961, p. 233; Benjamin Aaron and Michael I. Komaroff, "Statutory Regulations of Internal Union Affairs, II," *Illinois Law Review,* 44 (1949), p. 425; Sumner H. Slichter, James J. Healy, and E. Robert Livernash, *The Impact of Collective Bargaining on Management* (Washington: Brookings Institution, 1960), p. 41; Leo Bromwich, *Union Constitutions,* A Report to the Fund for the Republic (New York, 1959), p. 5; Jack Barbash, *The Practice of Unionism* (New York: Harper and Row, 1956), p. 172.

26. Barbash, *Labor's Grass Roots, loc. cit.,* Chapter V.

27. International Association of Machinists, *1964 Machinists Leadership School,* Section 4, Duties of Local Lodge Leaders.

28. Leiserson, *op. cit.,* p. 286.

29. See Barbash, *Labor's Grass Roots, loc. cit.,* Chapter V.

30. Institute of Labor and Industrial Relations, *Labor-Management Relations in Illini City,* Vol. 1 (Urbana: U. of Illinois, 1953), p. 682.

31. *Ibid.,* p. 571.

32. Parnes, *op. cit.,* p. 62.

33. Hjalmar Rosen and R. A. H. Rosen, "The Union Business Agent Looks at Collective Bargaining," *Personnel Magazine,* May 1957.

34. A. H. Raskin, "Labor's Welfare State, The New York Electrical Workers," *Atlantic Monthly*, April 1963.

35. See Arnold Rose, *Union Solidarity* (Minneapolis: U. of Minnesota Press, 1952); "Harold Gibbons—Hoffa's Left Hand," *The New Republic*, September 9, 1957; Barbash, *Labor's Grass Roots, loc. cit.*, pp. 82–84.

36. Michael Harrington, *The Retail Clerks* (New York: Wiley, 1962), pp. 46–53.

37. Barbash, *Practice of Unionism, loc. cit.*, pp. 384ff.

38. Barbash, *Labor's Grass Roots, loc. cit.*, pp. 93–99.

39. *Ibid.*, Chapter V.

40. Van Dusen Kennedy, *Nonfactory Unionism and Labor Relations* (Berkeley: U. of California Press, 1955).

CHAPTER IV—*The Local Union Substructure and the Union Member*

1. Herbert J. Lahne *et al.*, *Subunits of Local Unions: A Preliminary Analysis*, U.S. Dept. of Labor, BLMR (unpublished memorandum), 1960.

2. Joel Seidman *et al.*, *The Worker Views His Union* (Chicago: U. of Chicago Press, 1958), p. 272; *see also* Alice H. Cook, "Dual Government in Unions: A Tool for Analysis," *Industrial and Labor Relations Review*, April 1962.

3. Alice H. Cook, *Union Democracy: Practice and Ideal* (Ithaca: Cornell U. Press, 1963), p. 40.

4. *Ibid.* The first three of these locals have been studied in detail, but not identified as such. I have inferred the identification from internal evidence. In addition, see Jack Barbash, *Labor's Grass Roots* (New York: Harper and Row, 1961), pp. 69–71; and Maurice Neufeld, *Day In and Day Out with Local 3, IBEW* (Ithaca: Cornell U. Press, 1951), p. 1.

5. Cook, *Union Democracy: Practice and Ideal, loc. cit.*, p. 40.

6. *Ibid.*, p. 100.

7. Sidney and Beatrice Webb, *Industrial Democracy* (London: Longmans, Green, 1897).

8. "Due Process of Law," John R. Commons *Industrial Government* (New York: Macmillan, 1921), Chapter XVI, *passim.*

9. Sumner H. Slichter, *Union Policies and Industrial Management* (Washington: Brookings Institution, 1941), p. 2; *see also* Harold W. Davey, *Contemporary Collective*

Bargaining (Englewood Cliffs: Prentice-Hall, 1959), Chapter 9; and L. Reed Tripp, "The Union's Role in Industry—Its Extent and Limits," in IRRA, *Interpreting the Labor Movement* (Madison: IRRA, 1952).

10. Robert F. Hoxie, *Trade Unionism in the United States* (New York: Appleton, 1923), p. 265.

11. See Chapter XI for a discussion of union constitutionalism.

12. In general on stewards and grievance procedures see Jack Barbash, *The Practice of Unionism* (New York: Harper and Row, 1956), pp. 191–199 and *Labor's Grass Roots, loc. cit.*, Chapter 7; Frank Pierson, *Collective Bargaining Systems* (Washington: American Council on Public Affairs, 1942).

13. For the main types of grievance procedure provisions see U.S. Dept of Labor, Bureau of Labor Statistics, *Major Collective Bargaining Agreements: Grievance Procedures* (Washington: G.P.O., 1965), and Bureau of National Affairs, *Basic Patterns in Union Contracts* (Washington: BNA, 1961).

14. BLS, *Major Collective Bargaining Agreements: Grievance Procedures, loc. cit.*, p. 33.

15. *Ibid.*

16. Barbash, *Practice of Unionism, loc. cit.*, pp. 197–199.

17. Sidney M. Peck, *The Rank and File Leader* (New Haven: College and U. Press, 1963).

18. Barbash, *Labor's Grass Roots, loc. cit.*, Chapter 7.

19. Owen Tapper, *The Union Steward and How He Operates* (unpublished master's thesis), U. of Wisconsin, 1964, p. 50.

20. James W. Kuhn, *Bargaining in Grievance Settlement* (New York: Columbia U. Press, 1961).

21. *Ibid.*, pp. 53–55.

22. *Ibid.*, p. 47.

23. Lahne, *op. cit.*, pp. 12, 24.

24. Joseph Kovner and Herbert Lahne, "Shop Society and the Union," *Industrial and Labor Relations Review*, October 1953, pp. 7–8.

25. Tapper, *op. cit.*, pp. 56ff.

26. See pp. 15ff. above.

27. W. F. Whyte, *Money and Motivation* (New York: Harper and Row, 1955), p. 218. An uncommonly good summary of this school is to be found in Ametai Etzioni,

Modern Organizations (Englewood Cliffs: Prentice-Hall, 1964).

28. Kovner and Lahne, *op. cit.,* p. 4.

29. Seidman, *op. cit.,* pp. 195–196.

30. Clark Kerr and Abraham Siegel, "The Inter-Industry Propensity to Strike—An International Comparison," in Arthur Kornhauser *et al.,* eds., *Industrial Conflict* (New York: McGraw-Hill, 1954), pp. 191–195.

31. *Ibid.; see also* Thurman R. Lantz, *People of Coaltown* (New York: Columbia U. Press, 1958), p. 260; and Seidman, *op. cit.,* p. 24.

32. Leonard R. Sayles, *Behavior of Industrial Work Groups* (New York: Wiley, 1958), p. 93.

33. For a more extended treatment and the supporting literature see Barbash, *Labor's Grass Roots, loc. cit.,* Chapter 10.

34. Jack Barbash, "The Elements of Industrial Relations," *British Journal of Industrial Relations,* London, March 1964; Frederick I. Herzberg, Bernard Mausner and Barbara B. Snyderman, *The Motivation to Work* (New York: Wiley, 1959).

35. Hoxie, *op. cit.,* p. 263; *see also* Selig Perlman, *A Theory of the Labor Movement* (New York: Augustus M. Kelley, 1949 impression), Chapter VI.

36. *Ibid.,* p. 275.

CHAPTER V—*The Intermediate Body in Union Government*

1. I am substantially indebted to L.A. O'Donnell's *An Inquiry Into Union Structure—The Intermediate Body* (unpublished Ph.D. dissertation), U. of Wisconsin, Madison, 1961. *See also* Herbert Lahne's pioneering article, "The Intermediate Body in Collective Bargaining," *Industrial and Labor Relations Review,* January 1953; and William M. Leiserson, *American Trade Union Democracy* (New York: Columbia U. Press, 1959), Chapter XIII.

2. Morris A. Horowitz, *The New York Hotel Industry: A Labor Relations Study* (Cambridge: Harvard U. Press, 1960), pp. 70–71.

3. Jack Stieber, *Governing the UAW* (New York: Wiley, 1962), p. 100.

4. Lloyd Ulman, *The Government of the Steel Workers Union* (Englewood Cliffs: Prentice-Hall, 1959), p. 91.

5. O'Donnell, *op. cit.,* pp. 134–135.

6. *Ibid.*, pp. 158ff.

7. Ralph and Estelle James, series of articles on James Hoffa, *Industrial Relations*, May–October 1963.

8. Quoted *ibid.*, May 1963, p. 88, fn. 35.

9. Arnold Weber, ed., *Structure of Collective Bargaining* (New York: Free Press of Glencoe, 1961), p. 41.

10. A. H. Raskin, "Is Hoffa Finished?" *The Reporter*, March 26, 1964; "John E. Strong, 62, Teamster Leader," *New York Times* (obituary), June 16, 1965.

11. "Paper Unions Split Ranks," *Business Week*, June 6, 1964, p. 76; *see also The Rebel*, periodical of the Association of Western Pulp and Paper Workers, Portland, Oregon.

12. Weber, *op. cit.*, p. 40.

CHAPTER VI—*The National Union—Constitution and Convention*

1. Lloyd Ulman, *The Rise of the National Trade Union* (Cambridge: Harvard U. Press, 1955), pp. 3ff.; George E. Barnett, "The Dominance of the National Union in American Labor Organization," Vol. XXVII, *Quarterly Journal of Economics*, 1913, pp. 455–481; also in John R. Commons, ed., *Trade Unionism and Labor Problems* (Boston: Ginn, 1921).

2. J. B. Andrews, "Nationalization," in John R. Commons, *History of Labour in the United States*, Vol. II (New York: Macmillan, 1918), p. 43; *see also* John R. Commons, "American Shoemakers, 1648–1895," *Labor and Administration* (New York: Macmillan, 1923).

3. BLS, *Directory of National and International Unions in the United States, 1963* (Washington: G.P.O., 1963), p. iii.

4. Herbert J. Lahne, "The National Union in Federal Labor Legislation," *Labor Law Journal*, November 1963, p. 946.

5. See *ibid.* for the problems of definition.

6. BLS, *1963 Directory of National and International Labor Unions, loc. cit.*, p. 39.

7. *Ibid.*, p. 50.

8. Walton Hamilton, "Constitutionalism," *Encyclopedia of Social Science* (New York: Macmillan, 1931); William M. Leiserson, *American Trade Union Democracy* (New York: Columbia U. Press, 1959), pp. 108–109.

9. *Ibid.*, p. 98.

10. *Ibid.*, p. 106.

11. Herbert J. Lahne and Joseph Kovner, "Local Union Structure: Formality and Reality," *Industrial and Labor Relations Review,* October 1955, p. 26.

12. Herbert J. Lahne, "The Intermediate Union Body in Collective Bargaining," *Industrial and Labor Relations Review,* January 1953, p. 164.

13. Lahne and Kovner, *op. cit.,* p. 31.

14. Herbert S. Parnes, *Union Strike Votes* (Princeton: Princeton U., Industrial Relations Section, 1956), p. 67; George Strauss and Don Willner, *Government Regulation of Local Union Democracy,* in *Labor Law Journal,* N.Y. State School of Industrial and Labor Relations, Reprint Series, No. 18, August 1953.

15. See discussion in Chapter III.

16. U.S. Dept. of Labor, LMSA, *Union Constitutions and Election of Union Officers* (Washington: G.P.O., 1965), p. 7; U.S. Dept. of Labor, *Union Trusteeship* (Washington: G.P.O., 1962), pp. 97ff.; U.S. Dept. of Labor, Bureau of Labor Statistics, Bull. No. 1350, *Disciplinary Powers and Procedures in Union Constitutions* (Washington: G.P.O., 1963), Chapter VIII.

17. *The Rebel,* February 17, 1965, p. 9.

18. *The Rebel,* December 23, 1964, n.p.

19. Bureau of National Affairs, *Union Labor Report,* April 9, 1965, p. 4.

20. Leiserson, *op. cit.,* p. 110.

21. Ulman, *op. cit.,* Chapter V.

22. Theodore W. Glocker, *The Government of American Trade Unions* (Baltimore: Johns Hopkins, 1913), pp. 130–131; Ulman, *op. cit.,* Chapter II.

23. Leiserson, *op. cit.,* p. 87.

24. Frank T. Carlton, *History and Problems of Organized Labor* (Boston: Heath, 1911), pp. 96ff.; Leiserson, *op. cit.,* Chapters VII and VIII.

25. Hoxie, *Trade Unionism in the U.S.* (New York: Appleton, 1923), p. 120.

26. Glocker, *op. cit.,* pp. 199, 207.

27. National Industrial Conference Board, *Sourcebook of Union Government, Structure and Procedures* (New York: NICB, 1956), p. 73; *see also* Leo Bromwich, *Union Constitutions,* A Report to the Fund for the Republic (New York, 1959), p. 22.

28. Mark Perlman, *Democracy in the International Association of Machinists* (New York: Wiley, 1962), p. 82.

29. Leiserson, *op. cit.*, p. 217.

30. Morris A. Horowitz, *The Structure and Government of the Carpenters' Union* (New York: Wiley, 1962), p. 10.

31. *Ibid.*, pp. 10ff.

32. Leiserson, *op. cit.*, p. 123.

33. George Kozmetsky, *Financial Reports of Labor Unions* (Cambridge: Harvard Graduate School of Business, 1950).

34. Leiserson, *op. cit.*, pp. 127ff.; Bromwich, *op. cit.*, pp. 11–12.

35. Leiserson, *op. cit.*, p. 136.

36. NICB, *Handbook of Union Government, loc. cit.*, p. 78.

37. Joel Seidman, *The Brotherhood of Railroad Trainmen* (New York: Wiley, 1962), p. 165.

38. Melvin Rothbaum, *The Government of the Oil, Chemical, and Atomic Workers Union* (New York: Wiley, 1962), p. 103.

39. Bromwich, *op. cit.*, p. 13; Leiserson, *op. cit.*, p. 185.

40. Bromwich, *op. cit.*, p. 14.

41. NICB, *Handbook of Union Government, loc. cit.*, p. 71.

42. Rothbaum, *op. cit.*, p. 103.

43. BLS, *Disciplinary Powers and Procedures, loc. cit.*, p. 114.

44. *Ibid.*, p. 115; *see also* Jack Stieber, *Governing the UAW* (New York: Wiley, 1962), pp. 77–83; Harry R. Blaine and Frederick A. Zeller, "Who Uses the UAW Public Review Board?" *Industrial Relations,* Berkeley, May 1965 (see additional references therein).

45. NICB, *Handbook of Union Government, loc. cit.*, pp. 72ff.; Bromwich, *op. cit.*, pp. 22ff.

CHAPTER VII—*The National Union—Leadership and Administration*

1. National Industrial Conference Board, *Sourcebook of Union Government, Structure and Procedures* (New York: NICB, 1956), p. 85.

2. Melvin Rothbaum, *The Government of the Oil, Chemical, and Atomic Workers' Union* (New York: Wiley, 1962), pp. 65ff.

3. Philip Taft, "The Constitutional Power of the Chief Officer in American Labor Unions," *Quarterly Journal of Economics,* May 1948.

4. George Wood, *The Rebel,* December 23, 1964, p. 3; *see also* William M. Leiserson, *American Trade Union Democracy* (New York: Columbia U. Press, 1959), pp. 239ff.; Leo Bromwich, *Union Constitutions,* A Report to the Fund for the Republic (New York, 1959), pp. 20–21.

5. Morris A. Horowitz, *The Structure and Government of the Carpenters' Union* (New York: Wiley, 1962), pp. 10–15.

6. U.S. Dept. of Labor, Bureau of Labor Statistics, Bull. No. 1350, *Disciplinary Powers and Procedures in Union Constitutions* (Washington: G.P.O., 1963), p. 5.

7. *Ibid.,* p.6.

8. Philip Taft, *Structure and Government of Labor Unions* (Cambridge: Harvard U. Press, 1954), p. 180; *see also* Leiserson, *op. cit.,* pp. 267ff.; NICB, *Handbook of Union Government, loc. cit.,* pp. 69–71; Joel Seidman, *The Brotherhood of Railroad Trainmen* (New York: Wiley, 1962), pp. 83ff.; Clyde Summers, "Disciplinary Procedures of Unions," Vol. IV, No. 1, *Industrial and Labor Relations Review,* 1950, p. 19.

9. U.S. Dept. of Labor, BLMR, *Union Financial Statistics, 1959–60,* p. v, also Table 2.20.

10. *New York Times,* June 15, 1962, p. 12.

11. Albert Epstein (unpublished ms.), 1951.

12. Eric Peterson, "Administration of a National Union," in J. B. S. Hardman and Maurice Neufeld, eds., *The House of Labor* (New York: Prentice-Hall, 1951), p. 361.

13. Original LMRDA Financial Reports. On file in U.S. Dept. of Law, Washington, D.C.

14. Hardman and Neufeld, *The House of Labor, loc. cit.,* is the standard work on the practice of internal union administration. *See also* IRRA, *1957 Proceedings,* Part IX, "Current Intra-Union Research."

15. Russell Allen, "The Professional in Unions and His Educational Preparation," *Industrial and Labor Relations Review,* October 1962; Jack Barbash, "Leadership Within the Union," *Challenges to Labor Education in the 1960's* (Washington, D.C.: National Institute of Labor Education, 1962).

16. Doris K. Lewis, "Union Sponsored Middle-Income

Housing, 1927–65," *Monthly Labor Review,* July 1965, p. 629.

17. Florence Peterson, *American Labor Unions,* 2nd ed. (New York: Harper and Row, 1965), Chapter 13; Jack Barbash, "The Union and Negotiated Health and Welfare Plans," in H. Davey *et al.,* eds., *New Dimensions in Collective Bargaining* (New York: Harper and Row, 1959), pp. 105–108.

18. Harold M. Levinson, "Pattern Bargaining by the United Automobile Workers," *Labor Law Journal,* September 1958, pp. 672–673. A later version is to be found in "Pattern Bargaining: A Case Study of the Automobile Workers," *Quarterly Journal of Economics,* May 1960.

19. Horowitz, *op. cit.,* p. 50.

20. George Meany's testimony in U.S. Senate, Committee on Labor and Public Welfare, Subcommittee on Labor, *Union Financial and Administrative Practices and Procedures,* 8th Cong., 2nd Sess., pp. 63–65; Archibald Cox, "The Role of Law in Preserving Union Democracy," in *Labor in a Free Society* (Berkeley: U. of California Press, 1950), p. 77.

21. U.S. Dept. of Labor, *Union Trusteeship* (Washington: G.P.O., 1962), pp. 61, 68, 70; see Table 3.3, *ibid.,* p. 56, for detailed analysis.

22. *Ibid.,* p. 11; *see also* on trusteeship: Jack Barbash, *Labor's Grass Roots* (New York: Harper and Row, 1961), pp. 145–149; Arnold Weber, "Local Union Trusteeship and Public Policy," *Industrial and Labor Relations Review,* January 1961, p. 203.

23. NICB, *Handbook of Union Government, loc. cit.,* pp. 49–51 *passim.*

24. Robert R. France, *Union Decisions in Collective Bargaining* (Princeton: Princeton U. Press, Industrial Relations Section, 1955), pp. 21ff.

25. NICB, *Handbook of Union Government, loc. cit.,* p. 42; *Business Week,* August 8, 1959, p. 99.

26. U.S. Congress, Senate, *Union Financial and Administrative Practices and Procedures, op. cit.,* pp. 103–105.

27. Ralph and Estelle James, "Hoffa's Leverage and Techniques in Bargaining," *Industrial Relations,* October 1963.

28. Joel Seidman, *et al., The Worker Views His Union* (Chicago: U. of Chicago Press, 1958), p. 70.

29. Sidney M. Peck, *The Rank and File Leader* (New Haven: College and U. Press, 1963), pp. 63–64.

30. Paul H. Douglas, *Real Wages in the United States, 1890–1926* (New York: Houghton Mifflin, 1930), p. 564.

31. Gosta Rehn, "Unionism and Wage Structure in Sweden," in John T. Dunlop, ed., *The Theory of Wage Determination* (New York: St. Martin's, 1957), p. 228.

32. Richard A. Lester, "Revolution in Industrial Employment," *Labor Law Journal,* 1958; Arthur M. Ross, "New Concepts of Wage Determination," Vol. XIX, *NICB Management Record,* 1957.

33. Ralph and Estelle James, "Hoffa's Leverage and Techniques in Bargaining," *Industrial Relations,* October 1963; Sam Romer, *The International Brotherhood of Teamsters* (New York: Wiley, 1962), pp. 34ff.

34. James J. Healy, ed., *Creative Collective Bargaining* (Englewood Cliffs: Prentice-Hall, 1965), pp. 165ff.; Joseph P. Goldberg, *The Maritime Story: A Study in Labor-Management Relations* (Cambridge: Harvard U. Press, 1958).

35. Jack Barbash, *Unions and Telephones* (New York: Harper and Row, 1952).

36. Michael Harrington, *The Retail Clerks* (New York: Wiley, 1962), p. 42.

37. J. B. S. Hardman, "The Needle Trades Unions: A Labor Movement at Fifty," *Social Research,* Autumn 1960; *Fiftieth Anniversary Souvenir History of the New York Joint Board, ACWA, 1914–64* (New York, 1964), pp. 105–110.

38. See the following current materials: Murray Kempton, "Counted Out," *The New Republic,* April 24, 1965; *Business Week*: "Union Leaders Face Growing Revolt," October 3, 1964, pp. 54–56; "Political Row Perils Steel Peace," November 14, 1965, pp. 45–46; "Power Struggle Alters USW's Political Course," December 26, 1964, pp. 78–80; "The Man Steel Is Watching," March 27, 1965, p. 96; "Grassroots Militance in Steel," August 22, 1964, pp. 118–120; "UMW Faces a Miners' Revolt," August 15, 1964, pp. 101–2; "Another Union [OCAW] Changes the Guard," July 17, 1965, pp. 124–127; "Union Chiefs Face Double Trouble," December 12, 1964, pp. 99–100; *Wall Street Journal*: "Steel Worker War," January 5, 1965, p. 1; "McDonald Is Abel," January 26, 1965, p. 10; "Union Insurg-

ency," November 16, 1964, p. 14; U.S. Dept. of Labor, Office of Labor-Management and Welfare Reports, *Interim Report on Election of National President of International Union of Electrical and Machinery Workers* (IUE), Washington, April 5, 1965; A. H. Raskin, "Rumbles from the Rank and File," *The Reporter*, January 28, 1965, pp. 12–14.

39. Kempton, "Counted Out," *loc. cit.*, p. 16.

40. I have written about the altered collective bargaining climate of the 1957 period in: "The Impact of Technology on Labor–Management Relations," in G. Somers, ed., *Adjusting to Technological Change* (New York: Harper and Row, 1963), and "Union Response to the 'Hard Line,'" *Industrial Relations,* October 1961.

41. Lloyd Ulman, *The Government of the Steel Workers' Union* (Englewood Cliffs: Prentice-Hall, 1962), pp. 140ff.

CHAPTER VIII—*The AFL-CIO—The Government of a Federation*

1. In general the best source on the AFL-CIO are the *Reports of the AFL-CIO Executive Council* to the biennial convention.

2. Arthur J. Goldberg, *AFL-CIO: Labor United* (New York: McGraw-Hill, 1956), Chapter 2; Lewis L. Lorwin and Jean A. Flexner, *The American Federation of Labor: History, Policies and Prospects* (Washington: Brookings Institution, 1933).

3. BLS, *Directory of National and International Unions in the United States, 1963* (Washington: G.P.O., 1963), p. 42.

4. American Federation of Labor-Congress of Industrial Organizations, *Report of the Executive Council,* 1963, pp. 43–44.

5. Philip Taft, *The AFL From the Death of Gompers to the Merger* (New York: Harper and Row, 1959); Lorwin and Flexner, *op. cit.;* AFL-CIO *Executive Council Report,* 1963, pp. 286–384.

6. *Ibid.,* p. 10.

7. American Federation of Labor and Congress of Industrial Organizations, *Constitution,* December 1957, Art. X, Sec. 3.

8. AFL-CIO *Executive Council Report,* 1963, pp. 269–284.

9. David Dubinsky, quoted in Benjamin Stolberg, *Tailor's Progress* (New York: Doubleday, Doran, 1944), p. 276.

10. See discussion between Philip Taft and Leo Troy in "Local Independent Unions and the American Labor Movement," *Industrial and Labor Relations Review,* October 1961.

11. Jack Barbash, "Unions and Politics," *Challenge,* New York, December 1964; "The Structure of Union Political Action: A Trial Analytic Framework," Industrial Relations Research Association, Spring Meeting, 1965, *Labor Law Journal,* August 1965.

12. Andrew J. Biemiller, "Labor Issues in the 1960 Political Campaign: A Labor View," *Proceedings of the Thirteenth Annual Meeting,* Industrial Relations Research Association, 1960 (Madison, 1961), p. 218.

13. Alice H. Cook, "Labor's Search for Its Place in the Community," Vol. XXIX, No. 4, *Journal of Educational Sociology*; AFL-CIO *Executive Council Report,* 1963, pp. 158–162.

14. Jay Lovestone, "American Labor and the World Crisis," *1956 Proceedings,* Industrial Relations Research Association; John P. Windmuller, "ICFTU After Ten Years: Problems and Prospects," *Industrial and Labor Relations Review,* January 1961; AFL-CIO *Executive Council Report,* 1963, pp. 100–120; Philip Taft, *The AFL From the Death of Gompers, loc. cit.,* Chapters XIX, XXVII, XXVIII, XXIX; John Windmuller *American Labor and the International Labor Movement* (Ithaca: N.Y. State School of Industrial and Labor Relations, 1955); and Lewis Lorwin *The International Labor Movement* (New York: Harper and Row, 1953), provide the most systematic treatment of labor's role in international affairs.

15. "Union Spends Millions on Foreign Aid Programs," *Business Week,* August 24, 1963.

16. "Expanded Aid Pledged to Free African Unions," *AFL-CIO News,* March 6, 1965, p. 4.

17. "ICFTU—Estimate and Perspective," *AFL-CIO Free Trade Union News,* June 1965, p. 1.

18. John D. Pomfret, "Lovestone Gets High Labor Post," *New York Times,* December 21, 1963.

19. "Labor Man of the World," *New York Times,* December 21, 1963. *See also* Sidney Lens, "Lovestone Diplomacy," *The Nation,* July 5, 1965.

20. " 'On Strike' Against the World," *New York Times* (editorial), April 12, 1964; "Labor Takes a Harder Line Overseas," *Business Week*, April 24, 1965; "Union Spends Millions on Foreign Aid Programs," *Business Week*, August 24, 1963.

21. Walter Galenson, *The CIO Challenge to the AFL* (Cambridge: Harvard U. Press, 1960); Philip Taft, *The AFL in the Time of Gompers* (New York: Harper and Row, 1957), Chapter VI.

22. AFL-CIO *Executive Council Report*, 1963, pp. 58ff.

23. AFL-CIO *Milwaukee Labor Press*, September 9, 1965, p. 3; *see also* Doris K. Lewis, "Union Sponsored Middle-Income Housing, 1927–65," *Monthly Labor Review*, July 1965.

24. "AFL-CIO Shuns Hutcheson Issue," *New York Times*, February 21, 1959.

25. Max Kampelman, *The Communist Party vs. the CIO* (New York: Praeger, 1957); Congress of Industrial Organizations, *Expulsion of Communist Dominated Organizations*, Pamphlet No. 254 (Washington: CIO, 1954).

26. AFL-CIO, *Constitution, loc. cit.*, Art. II, Sec. 4.

27. Statement of George Meany, President, AFL-CIO, before the Special Subcommittee on Labor of the House Committee on Education and Labor, on the Equal Employment Opportunities Bills (mimeographed), January 24, 1962, p. 6.

28. Tom Brooks, "The Negro's Place at Labor's Table," *The Reporter*, December 6, 1962, pp. 38ff.

29. George Meany, Address, AFL-CIO, April 13, 1965.

30. Ray Marshall, *The Negro and Organized Labor* (New York: Wiley, 1965), p. 81.

31. Quoted *ibid.*, p. 238.

32. For example, A. H. Raskin, "Labor and Civil Rights," *New York Times*, May 20, 1964.

33. Herbert Hill, "Racial Inequality in Employment: The Patterns of Discrimination," *The Annals*, American Academy of Political and Social Science, January 1965, p. 30.

34. Goldberg, *op. cit.*, pp. 143–145; pp. 228–231.

35. "Text of New Internal Disputes Plan," *AFL-CIO News*, Washington, December 23, 1961, p. 6; *see also* AFL-CIO *Executive Council Report*, 1963, pp. 51–52.

36. Jack Barbash, "Jurisdiction," *Industrial Bulletin*, N.Y. State Dept. of Labor, November 1957.

CHAPTER IX—*Power and Influence Within the AFL-CIO*

1. There is no full-dress treatment of Meany. A. H. Raskin has followed Meany's career in a number of articles, all in the *New York Times Magazine:* "New Task for Blunt Meany," February 20, 1955; "Crusader for Clean Unionism," October 20, 1957; "Labor's House Three Years After," November 30, 1958.

2. A. H. Raskin, "Meany and Reuther—Uneasy Togetherness," *New York Times Magazine,* April 5, 1959.

3. Sam Romer, *The International Brotherhood of Teamsters* (New York: Wiley, 1926); and Ralph and Estelle James' series on Hoffa, *Industrial Relations,* May–October 1963, are the best treatments of Hoffa.

4. John D. Pomfret, "Lovestone Gets High Labor Post," *New York Times,* December 21, 1963.

5. David J. Saposs, "Voluntarism in the American Labor Movement," *Monthly Labor Review,* September 1954.

CHAPTER X—*Inside Politics of the Union*

1. Bernard Crick, *In Defense of Politics* (Baltimore: Penguin, 1964), p. 30. This work has been generally influential in the design of this chapter.

2. Arnold P. Weber, "The Craft-Industrial Issue Revisited: A Study of Union Government," *Industrial and Labor Relations Review,* April 1963.

3. *Ibid.*

4. James W. Kuhn, *Bargaining in Grievance Settlement* (New York: Columbia U. Press, 1961), p. 139.

5. George W. Taylor, "Collective Bargaining in Transition," in Arnold Weber, ed., *Structure of Collective Bargaining* (New York: Free Press of Glencoe, 1961), p. 349.

6. Stanley Weir, "The ILWU: A Case Study in Bureaucracy–II," Vol. III, No. 3, *New Politics,* p. 62; *see also ibid.,* Part I, Vol. III, No. 1.

7. Federal Conciliation and Mediation Service, *Annual Report* (Washington: G.P.O., 1962), p. 5; A. H. Raskin, "Rumbles from the Rank and File," *The Reporter,* January 28, 1965.

8. Jack Barbash, *Unions and Telephones* (New York: Harper and Row, 1952).

9. Leo Kramer, *Labor's Paradox: The American Federation of State, County, and Municipal Employees* (New York: Wiley, 1962), p. 116.

10. Ralph and Estelle James' series on Hoffa, *Industrial Relations*, May–October 1963, p. 88.

11. Scott Greer, *Last Man In* (New York: Free Press of Glencoe, 1959), pp. 41ff.; Jack Barbash, *Labor's Grass Roots* (New York: Harper and Row, 1961), pp. 172–173; Jack Barbash, "Ethnic Factors in the Development of the American Labor Movement," in IRRA, *Interpreting the Labor Movement* (Madison: IRRA, 1952).

12. Sam Romer, *The International Brotherhood of Teamsters* (New York: Wiley, 1962), p. 49.

13. Barbash, *Labor's Grass Roots, loc. cit.*, pp. 175–176 *passim*.

14. Max Kampelman, *The Communist Party vs. The CIO* (New York: Praeger, 1957); David J. Saposs, *Communism in American Unions* (New York: McGraw–Hill, 1959).

15. Michael Harrington, "Catholics in the Labor Movement: A Case History," *Labor History*, Fall 1960, pp. 259–261 *passim;* Philip Taft, "The Association of Catholic Trade Unionists," *Industrial and Labor Relations Review*, January 1949, p. 218.

16. *Webster's Third New International Dictionary*, 1961.

17. Matthew Woll, quoted in Bernard Karsh, *Membership Control of Trade Unions: Some Contingencies*, paper for delivery at IRRA Conference (mimeographed), May 1958, p. 3.

18. *Ibid.*

19. Crick, *op. cit.*, p. 62.

20. Leo Bromwich, *Union Constitutions*, A Report to the Fund for the Republic (New York, 1959), p. 37.

21. Seymour M. Lipset *et. al.*, *Union Democracy* (New York: Free Press of Glencoe, 1956).

22. Barbash, *Labor's Grass Roots, loc. cit.*, pp. 182–183.

23. Jack Steiber, *Governing the UAW* (New York: Wiley, 1962), pp. 67–72.

24. Kuhn, *op. cit.*, p. 145; *see also* Leonard R. Sayles, *Behavior of Industrial Work Groups* (New York: Wiley, 1958).

25. Neil Chamberlain, *The Union Challenge to Manage-*

ment Control (New York: Harper, 1948), p. 277; Kuhn, *op. cit.*

26. Robert S. Gallagher and Ronald Semple, "The Life and Times of Tony Pro," *The Reporter,* September 12, 1963, pp. 16–17.

27. Ray Marshall, *The Negro and Organized Labor* (New York: Wiley, 1965), pp. 68–73.

28. Barbash, *Labor's Grass Roots, loc. cit.,* pp. 188–189.

29. Seymour M. Lipset, *Political Man* (New York: Doubleday-Anchor, 1964), p. 1.

30. Barbash, *Labor's Grass Roots, loc. cit.,* pp. 66–69.

31. Garth L. Mangum, *The Operating Engineers* (Cambridge: Harvard U. Press, 1964); National Industrial Conference Board, *Sourcebook, Structure and Procedures of Union Government* (New York: NICB, 1956), p. 80.

32. U.S. Dept. of Labor, Labor–Management Services Administration, *Summary of Operations* (annual).

33. Bernard Samoff, "The Impact of Taft–Hartley Job Discrimination Victories," *Industrial Relations,* May 1965; *see also* Bernard Samoff's *Union-Caused Employee Discrimination Under the Taft–Hartley Act* (unpublished Ph.D. dissertation), U. of Pennsylvania, 1963.

34. Gallagher and Semple, "The Life and Times of Tony Pro," *op. cit.;* Robert F. Kennedy, *The Enemy Within* (New York: Harper and Row, 1960), pp. 120ff.

35. Robert A. Dahl, *A Preface to Democratic Theory* (Chicago: U. of Chicago Press, 1956), p. 145.

36. Arthur M. Ross, *Trade Union Wage Policy* (Berkeley: U. of California Press, 1950), p. 12.

CHAPTER XI—*The Union as a Government—
A Summing-Up*

General note: Since this chapter is recapitulative, there will be little noting other than direct quotations and significant books not cited earlier.

1. Sidney and Beatrice Webb, *The History of Trade Unionism,* new edition (London: Longmans, Green, 1920), p. 41.

2. C. F. Strong, *Modern Political Constitutions* (London: Sedgwick and Jackson, 1958), p. 61.

3. *Ibid.*

4. Peter M. Blau, *Bureaucracy in Modern Society* (New York: Random House, 1964), p. 19.

5. A. D. Lindsay, *The Modern Democratic State*, Vol. I (London: Oxford U. Press, 1943), p. 282.

6. *Ibid.*

7. Robert A. Dahl, *A Preface to Democratic Theory* (Chicago: U. of Chicago Press, 1956), p. 145.

8. George Brooks, *The Sources of Vitality in the American Labor Movement* (Ithaca: Cornell U. Press, N.Y. State School of Industrial and Labor Relations, 1960), p. 29.

9. National Labor Relations Board, *Twenty–Eighth Annual Report* (Washington: G.P.O., 1964), Table 13A, p. 178.

10. Arnold R. Weber, "Competitive Unionism in the Chemical Industry," *Industrial and Labor Relations Review*, October 1959, p. 35; *see also* Joseph Krislov, "Organizational Rivalry Among American Unions," *Industrial and Labor Relations Review*, January 1960.

11. U.S. Dept. of Labor, Bureau of Labor Standards, *State Labor Relations Acts, January 1961* (Washington: G.P.O., 1961), pp. 7ff.

12. V. I. Lenin, *What Is To Be Done* (New York: International Publishers, 1929), p. 77.

13. Walter Lippmann, *Drift and Mastery* (Englewood Cliffs: Prentice-Hall, 1961), p. 62.

14. Sidney and Beatrice Webb, *Industrial Democracy*, Vol. I (London: Longmans, Green, 1897), p. 8.

15. William M. Leiserson, *American Trade Union Democracy* (New York: Columbia U. Press, 1959), p. 286.

16. Lenin, *op. cit.*, p. 131.

17. Frank Tannenbaum, *A Philosophy of Labor* (New York: Knopf, 1951), Chapter V.

18. Sidney and Beatrice Webb, Vol. I, *Industrial Democracy, loc. cit.*, p. 140.

19. Thomas G. Spates, *Human Values Where People Work* (New York: Harper and Row, 1960), pp. 164–165 *passim*.

20. Raymond Williams, *Culture and Society* (New York: Doubleday-Anchor, 1960), p. 346.

INDEX